HOT WORDS FOR THE SAT*

THE 350 WORDS YOU NEED TO KNOW

by MURRAY BROMBERG and JULIUS LIEBB

*"Scholastic Aptitude Test" and "SAT" are registered trademarks of the College Entrance Examination Board. This book was prepared by Barron's Educational Series, Inc., which is solely responsible for its contents. It is not endorsed by any other organization.

BARRON'S

New York • London • Toronto • Sydney

All inquiries should be addressed to:
Barron's Educational Series, Inc.
250 Wireless Boulevard
Hauppauge, New York 11788

Library of Congress Catalog Card No. 88-34272

International Standard Book No. 0-8120-4120-8

Library of Congress Cataloging-in-Publication Data

Bromberg, Murray.
Hot words for the SAT.

1. Scholastic aptitude test—Study guides.
2. Vocabulary. I. Liebb, Julius.   II. Title.
LB2353.57.B75   1989   378'.1664   88-34272
ISBN 0-8120-4120-8

PRINTED IN THE UNITED STATES OF AMERICA

901 800 987654321

CONTENTS

Lesson 10/Page 40
diminution   discerning   disdain   dismantle   disparage
disparity   disperse   disposition   dissipated   distraught

Review Exercises: Lessons 6–10/Page 44

Lesson 11/Page 47
dogmatic   dormant   duplicity   ebb   eclectic   efface
effervescent   egregious   elucidate   elusive

Lesson 12/Page 51
embellish   embroil   emulate   enervate   engender
enhance   enigma   ephemeral   equanimity   equivocate

Lesson 13/Page 55
esoteric   eulogy   euphemism   evanescent   exacerbate
exemplary   expedient   expedite   expunge   extol

Lesson 14/Page 59
facilitate   fallacy   fastidious   fervor   fitful   flagrant
fledgling   forlorn   formidable   fortuitous

Lesson 15/Page 63
furtive   galvanize   garbled   garner   garrulous   gratuitous
guile   gullible   hackneyed   haphazard

Review Exercises: Lessons 11–15/Page 67

Lesson 16/Page 70
hedonist   heretic   hierarchy   homogeneous   hyperbole
hypocritical   hypothetical   iconoclast   immaterial   imminent

Lesson 17/Page 74
immutable   impartial   impassive   imperturbable   implausible
inadvertent   incipient   incisive   incongruous   incontrovertible

Lesson 18/Page 78
incorrigible   indefatigable   indigent   ingratiate   innocuous
inscrutable   insipid   insurgent   intemperate   intractable

Lesson 19/Page 82
irrefutable   irrelevant   jargon   judicious   kindle   labyrinth
lackluster   laconic   lampoon   lassitude

Lesson 20/Page 86
latent   laudable   lethargic   levity   listless   lucid
malicious   marred   meager   meandering

Review Exercises: Lessons 16–20/Page 90

Lesson 21/Page 93
meticulous   mitigate   morose   nomenclature   nonchalance
obliterate   obscure   obsolete   officious   opportunist

Lesson 22/Page 98
opulent   overt   painstaking   pariah   parsimonious
partisan   paucity   peerless   perceptive   perfidy

Lesson 23/Page 102
peripheral   peruse   philistine   piety   pique   placate
placid   plagiarize   platitude   pompous

Lesson 24/Page 107
ponderous   pragmatic   preclude   precocious   prestigious
pretentious   procrastinate   prodigious   profane   profusion

Lesson 25/Page 111
prolific   propensity   provincial   prudent   pugnacious
quandary   querulous   quixotic   raconteur   rancor

Review Exercises: Lessons 21–25/Page 115

Lesson 26/Page 118
raze   rebuff   recalcitrant   recluse   redundant   refurbish
rejuvenate   relegate   relic   remorse

Lesson 27/Page 122
repudiate   repugnant   rescind   residual   resilient   respite
reticent   retract   ruthless   sagacious

Lesson 28/Page 126
salutary   sanction   saturate   savory   scapegoat   scoff
scrupulous   scrutinize   sectarian   sequester

Lesson 29/Page 131
serene   skeptical   sobriety   solemn   soporific   sporadic
spurious   squalid   stagnate   stoic

INTRODUCTION

"I need to raise my SAT verbal score, but who has the time to study 20,000 words!"

That's a familiar complaint from students who recognize the importance of a rich vocabulary but are overwhelmed by the logistics of test preparation. We reasoned that typical high school students need guidance to make every minute of vocabulary study a productive one. After all, why waste time reviewing words such as *optimistic* or *traitor* which you already know, or squander precious moments puzzling over esoteric words such as *syzygy* or *tergiversate* which will never be tested?

However, between those extremes are thousands of frequently used vocabulary words of a level of difficulty which has been embraced by the test-makers. With the aid of computers, we have examined all of the words used on the released editions of the SAT and chosen a favorite 350 which turn up with a high degree of regularity, year after year.

By mastering this narrow group of "winners," you will be ready to earn a higher score on the verbal portion of the SAT you take.

Using This Book Efficiently

This book is divided into 35 lessons, each with 10 vocabulary words. Most students find they can do justice to one lesson in 30-45 minutes. We suggest you start by covering the first definition with your hand, and seeing whether you can compose one on your own. Next, read the three model sentences to see how the word is used in context. (Reading aloud is highly recommended.) Continue doing this for each new word in the lesson.

Next, study the "Spotlight On" words, which is a good way to develop an interest in word origins, as well as to stretch your vocabulary. Then, do the Matching exercise, which will fix additional synonyms in your mind. The remaining exercises (Fill in the Blanks and True or False) are designed to reinforce what you have learned. Check your work with the Answer Key, making sure to review those words that gave you trouble. We also suggest that you write two original sentences for each new word, since that is one of the best ways to make a word part of your permanent expanded vocabulary.

In addition to the 35 lessons, there are review sections after every five lessons. These sections contain analogy and antonym questions similar to those on the SAT, as well as an exercise called "Headlines," all of which will allow you to demonstrate your mastery of the new words. By the time you complete each series of five lessons and the reviews, you will have been exposed to each of the "hot" words at least five or six times. Such repetition and reinforcement are critical to vocabulary study.

If you are preparing for a specific SAT date, plan a study schedule based on how much time you have before the test. If, for example, you have about ten weeks to study, you might concentrate on three lessons each week. By learning those thirty words systematically every week, you will be better prepared when you open your test booklet on the important day.

Murray Bromberg
Julius Liebb

LESSON 1

- aberration ▪ abstinence ▪ abstract ▪ acclaim ▪ acquiesce
- admonish ▪ advocate ▪ aesthetic ▪ affinity ▪ aggrandizement

aberration *n.* a deviating from the right path or usual course of action; a mental disorder, especially of a minor or temporary nature.

We were convinced that Ed's poor test marks were an *aberration*, and that he would do better the next time.

The scientists looked for a possible *aberration* in the laboratory animal's behavior after administering the experimental drug.

Sandra's father's forgetfulness was not an isolated *aberration* but the onset of Alzheimer's disease.

abstinence *n.* the giving up of certain pleasures such as food or drink.

After years of indulgence, it was difficult for Eric to follow his doctor's directive of complete *abstinence* from liquor.

Myra's *abstinence* from cake, candy, and ice cream led to a dramatic weight loss.

I believed the alcoholic would soon forget his pledge of *abstinence*.

abstract *adj.* theoretical, not applied or practical; not concrete; hard to understand. (As a noun, abstract means "a summary.")

I prefer realistic art to *abstract* paintings which are totally confusing to me.

To him, hunger was an *abstract* concept, having never missed a meal himself.

The original document was sixty pages long, so I appreciated Sid's concise *abstract*.

acclaim *n.* loud applause; approval. (When used as a verb, acclaim means "to applaud; to praise.")

Jonas Salk won great *acclaim* for his medical discoveries.

With *acclaim* ringing in his ears, the champion left the ring.

The minister intended to *acclaim* the philanthropist at his funeral.

acquiesce *v.* to accept the conclusions or arrangements of others; to accede; to give consent by keeping silent.

The president said that we will never *acquiesce* to the demands of terrorists.

Although many members were critical about the issue, when it came to a vote they *acquiesced*.

When the merchant saw that we were ready to *acquiesce*, he rubbed his hands with great glee.

admonish *v.* to advise against something; to warn; to scold gently; to urge strongly.

This is the last time I plan to *admonish* you about coming late to work.

Uncle Jack never failed to *admonish* my cousins about their poor table manners.

The Holocaust survivor *admonished* the audience with his closing words, "Never again!"

advocate *v.* to support; to be in favor of. (When used as a noun, advocate refers to someone who supports a particular cause.)

He *advocates* higher salaries for teachers, hoping competitive pay scales will make the teaching profession more attractive to college students.

Because the candidate plans to *advocate* many new social programs, he is being called a big spender.

The foreign minister, who until recently supported military stockpiling, has now become an *advocate* of total disarmament.

aesthetic *adj.* showing an appreciation of beauty in nature or art; artistic.

Kyra's *aesthetic* qualities were apparent in her early art work.

The so-called Ashcan School of artists found *aesthetic* merit in ordinary city scenes.

My *aesthetic* sense was revolted by Harriette's choice of wallpaper.

affinity *n.* natural attraction to a person or liking for a thing; relation; connection.

Harvey's *affinity* for math led him to excel in our computer course.

In Prof. Carlson's oil painting class I developed an *affinity* for aesthetic values.

The couple's *affinity* was attested to by fifty happy years together.

aggrandizement *n.* an increase in rank or wealth; growth in power.

I attributed Paul's aggressiveness to his need for *aggrandizement*.

The United Nations refused to acquiesce to the dictator's desire for self-*aggrandizement*.

Wall Street raiders sometimes get burned in their quest for *aggrandizement*.

SPOTLIGHT ON

acclaim The word *clamor* means "loud uproar." It has the same Latin origin as *acclaim*; both come from a verb meaning "to cry out."

affinity *affinitás* means "related by marriage." Having an affinity for something indicates a strong relationship (art, languages, scuba diving, etc.) even without the bonds of matrimony.

MATCHING

Match the words in Column A with their meanings in Column B.

A	B
1. aberration	a. warn
2. abstinence	b. growth in power
3. abstract	c. unusual course of action
4. acclaim	d. critical
5. acquiesce	e. staying away from alcohol
6. admonish	f. attraction
7. advocate	g. be in favor of
8. aesthetic	h. not concrete
9. affinity	i. artistic
10. aggrandizement	j. accede
	k. approval

FILL IN THE BLANK

Use the new words in the following sentences.

1. My _____ for detective stories led me naturally to the Sherlock Holmes collection.

2. Network executives were forced to _____the talk show host about his language.

3. We could only hope that Fred's cruelty was a temporary _____.

4. I find it hard to decipher modern poetry because it's so _____.

5. I'll _____ about the summer vacation if you give in concerning winter recess.

6. To great _____, the actress mounted the stage to accept her Oscar.

7. Upon entering the monastery, he was sworn to an oath of verbal _____.

8. Those who _____ violence must be prepared to take responsibility for their actions.

9. In the 1980s, Russia was accused of _____ in its conflict with Afghanistan.

10. I found the black canvas completely devoid of _____ excellence.

TRUE OR FALSE

Based upon the way the new words are used, identify the following sentences as True (T) or False (F).

1. As an artist, he was starved for acclaim but that came long after his death.

2. If you acquiesce to our request, we'll compensate you generously.

3. I'm an advocate of raising the minimum wage because I think workers are overpaid now.

4. Although the painting lacked aesthetic qualities, it was true to life.

5. Having an affinity for the downtrodden, Shelly became a social worker.

LESSON 2

alienate *v.* to turn away the normal feelings of fondness toward anyone; to estrange.

Unwilling to *alienate* our old neighbors, we put up with their boisterous friends.

Rory admonished his son by saying that continued lateness would *alienate* his boss.

By abrogating its responsibilities, the French government threatened to *alienate* its supporters in the United States.

alleviate *v.* to make easier to endure; to relieve; to diminish.

Nothing tends to *alleviate* my headaches better than simple aspirin.

Although the new drug is said to *alleviate* the symptoms, it will not cure the disease.

We hired two new secretaries to *alleviate* the office work load.

aloof *adj.* indifferent; unsympathetic; not interested; apart.

She was adamant about remaining *aloof* from family problems.

Some teachers are genuinely interested in their students' lives, but others prefer to stand *aloof*.

Formerly cold and *aloof*, Regina surprised us with her new openness.

altruistic *adj.* thoughtful of the welfare of others.

Arthur's natural *altruistic* affinity endeared him to one and all.

Scrooge's new *altruistic* attitude redeemed him for Dickens's readers.

Under pressure, the corporate president reluctantly acquiesced and adopted an *altruistic* policy toward the employees.

ambiguous *adj.* permitting more than one interpretation; not clearly defined.

5

Listening to Archer's *ambiguous* remarks, we weren't sure whether he was on our side.

Politicians are often fond of *ambiguous* statements which won't alienate certain blocs of voters.

Because there was nothing *ambiguous* about Blanche's philosophy, we knew at all times where she stood on discrimination.

ambivalence *n.* condition of having conflicting attitudes.

The manager's *ambivalence* toward his star outfielder confused the sportswriters.

Mel's *ambivalence*, his lack of a clearcut position, was irritating.

Senator Todd changed his mind so often that he became notorious for his *ambivalence*.

ameliorate *v.* to make better or more tolerable; to improve.

In an effort to *ameliorate* the marriage relationship, the alcoholic agreed to a one-year period of abstinence.

Ernie's apology is sure to *ameliorate* the situation.

A new lavatory was installed in order to *ameliorate* working conditions.

analogous *adj.* similar in certain qualities; comparable.

The auto mechanic said that the engine was *analogous* to the human heart.

A dictator's desire for territorial aggrandizement is hardly *analogous* to my wishes for a cabin in the Poconos.

When Lloyd said that my appetite was *analogous* to a vulture's, our friendship was abrogated.

animosity *n.* active dislike; ill will.

The immigrants were faced with *animosity* when they moved into our neighborhood.

My *animosity* toward boxing is a result of my pacificistic upbringing.

Expecting that Molly would show *animosity*, I was surprised by her warm acceptance of my new plan.

anonymity *n.* condition of being nameless or unknown.

Some philanthropists crave the spotlight, but Edith preferred *anonymity* for her altruism.

After two decades of *anonymity*, Ellis acquiesced to putting his real name on his new novel.

Previous Russian leaders have chosen *anonymity* for their families and personal lives.

SPOTLIGHT ON

ambiguous Knowing that the prefix *ambi* means *"around, in two ways"* can help us to decipher a number of good SAT words such as *ambiance, ambidextrous, ambient, amble, ambulant.* Can you define them?

analogous Each of our review sections contains analogy exercises which incorporate our vocabulary words. The Greek words *analogous*, "proportionate," and *analogon*, "according to due ration," help to explain why analogous means "similar in certain qualities."

MATCHING

Match the words in Column A with their meaning in Column B.

A	B
1. alienate	a. concerned about others
2. alleviate	b. unclear
3. aloof	c. to improve
4. altruistic	d. estrange
5. ambiguous	e. spryness
6. ambivalence	f. reserved
7. ameliorate	g. remaining unknown
8. analogous	h. with conflicting attitudes
9. animosity	i. comparable
10. anonymity	j. active dislike
	k. relieve

FILL IN THE BLANK

Use the new words in the following sentences.

1. Accused of _____, the mayor was urged to clarify his position on the death penalty.

2. It's ironic that some successful actors ultimately long for _____.

3. Having no desire to _____ his friends, Andy invited more people to the wedding than he could afford.

4. The black poet was criticized for having remained _____ from civil rights protests.

5. Getting fired was _____ to being hit in the stomach.

6. Barry's sudden _____ deeds didn't deceive us about his true character.

7. When she realized that Roger showed extreme _____ to regular discipline, Mrs. Bryant referred him to the Guidance Department.

8. The criticism of my essay was so _____ that I didn't know what kind of mark to expect.

9. Shall I use a heating pad or an ice pack to _____ the pain?

10. When we reached an impasse, an arbitrator was inivited to _____ the matter.

TRUE OR FALSE

Based upon the way the new words are used, identify the following sentences as True (T) or False (F).

1. The new medication is said to be able to alleviate a migraine headache within minutes.

2. Leonard's ambiguous response was appreciated because we then knew where he stood.

3. Many shy people prefer anonymity to the spotlight.

4. If you alienate her affections, she might sue for divorce.

5. The truly altruistic philanthropist refused to take credit for helping the poor families.

LESSON 3

antagonism *n.* hostility, active opposition.

Teenagers sometimes show *antagonism* toward parental sugges-tions that they clean up their rooms.

Terry's *antagonism* was displayed by his refusal to be objective about our proposal.

The manager's *antagonism* toward my plan vanished as soon as he saw our increase in profits.

antithesis *n.* direct opposite.

Surprisingly, Donna is the *antithesis* of her twin, Debby.

The Democrats' election platform was the *antithesis* of the Repub-licans'.

What Shana did was the *antithesis* of what she had promised to do.

apochryphal *adj.* of doubtful authenticity; counterfeit.

Her *apochryphal* tears fooled no one.

The story of George Washington and the cherry tree is *apochryphal,* no doubt.

Despite our suspicions that the incident was *apochryphal,* we em-braced it eagerly as being truthful.

arduous *adj.* hard to do; strenuous.

Climbing Mt. Everest is an *arduous* undertaking.

Until Hercules accomplished it, cleaning the Augean Stables was considered an *arduous* task.

We ended our basic training with an *arduous* forced march through the swamps.

articulate *adj.* able to put one's thoughts into words easily and clearly. (When articulate is used as a verb, it means "to speak dis-tinctly.")

Being *articulate*, Ellyn was able to do well on her job interviews.

Mr. Montero hardly expected the kindergartner to be so *articulate*.

Try to *articulate* clearly when you read the poem aloud.

assuage *v.* to calm or soothe; to satisfy.

Mother hastened to the bedroom to *assuage* Beth's fears.

Dr. Zilka was able to *assuage* the nervous patient with an optimistic diagnosis.

Many athletes drink Gatorade to *assuage* their thirst.

atrophy *v.* to waste away.

Failure to exercise your muscles may cause them to *atrophy*.

Our teacher was fond of saying that one's commonsense could *atrophy* if it's not used.

Tracy expected her leg to *atrophy* after it had been in a cast for two months.

augment *v.* to increase or enlarge; to become greater in size.

If we *augment* our arms stockpile, the Russians will do the same.

The factory plans to *augment* the basic work force with some part-time employees.

You can augment your income by working overtime.

austere *adj.* stern in manner or appearance; strict in morals.

Their household, governed by an *austere* father, was a humorless and unhappy place.

When the *austere* lifestyle proved to be too arduous to maintain, Alberto left the monastery.

Expecting that our week with an Amish family would be an *austere* experience, we were pleasantly surprised by the lavish meals.

authoritarian *n.* a person who supports the principle of subjection to authority instead of individual freedom. (This word is also used as an adjective.)

The rebel colonel claimed to have an affinity for democracy, but we knew that he was an *authoritarian* through and through.

As the family *authoritarian*, my eldest brother succeeded in alienating the rest of us.

The permissive Ms. Sharett is the antithesis of the *authoritarian* Ms. Robins.

SPOTLIGHT ON

apochryphal The Apochrypha is the name given to certain early Christian writing which was excluded from the New Testament. To tell an apochryphal story today is to relate an anecdote which is probably not authentic.

austere *Austere* is derived from a Greek word that means "dry." Someone who was excessively stern in manner, severe and self-disciplined, might have appeared dried up to the ancients.

MATCHING

Match the words in Column A with their meanings in Column B.

A	B
1. antagonism	a. to calm
2. antithesis	b. direct opposite
3. apochryphal	c. waste away
4. arduous	d. add to
5. articulate	e. fictitious
6. assuage	f. stern
7. atrophy	g. one who favors blind submission to authority
8. augment	h. difficult
9. austere	i. of an era
10. authoritarian	j. hostility
	k. able to speak well

FILL IN THE BLANK

Use the new words in the following sentences.

1. Unwilling to allow his brain to _____, the prisoner composed a daily newspaper in his mind.

2. In an attempt to _____ the irate family, the landlord lowered their rent.

3. We voted Vaughn out of office when it became apparent that he was an _____.

4. Harold, constantly ordered around by his boss, resented such _____ behavior.

11

5. Bob's _____ melted away after he was presented with the facts.

6. One of Victor's problems is that he accepts as gospel all of the _____ stories he hears.

7. My latest essay, the _____ of the first one I submitted, received an "A."

8. Claiming that extracting the impacted tooth would be too _____ an undertaking for him, my dentist referred me to a specialist.

9. To _____ his salary, Ira did freelance editing.

10. A used car salesman needs to be _____ if he's to be successful.

TRUE OR FALSE

Based upon the way the new words are used, identify the following sentences as True (T) or False (F).

1. Abandoning their ancient antagonism, the heads of both families shook hands.

2. James said that the anecdote was apochryphal, and that's why we believed it to be absolutely genuine.

3. Unloading the truckload of coal was extremely arduous work.

4. By selling cosmetics door to door, Ellie was able to augment her widow's pension.

5. One of the highest tributes we could pay to the liberal, sensitive jurist was to call him authoritarian.

Lesson 4

■ autonomy ■ aversion ■ belittle ■ bequeath ■ bizarre ■ blithe
■ bombastic ■ buffoon ■ cache ■ cacophony

autonomy *n.* independence, self-government.

In search of *autonomy*, the settlers refused to pay taxes to their mother country.

Greater *autonomy* was the candidate's promise, should he be elected.

Since the judge was an authoritarian, the lawyers could not look for any *autonomy* in his court.

aversion *n.* strong or fixed dislike; antipathy.

Having an *aversion* toward cheese, I avoid eating pizza.

Coach Grady has an *aversion* toward players who are unwilling to pass the ball.

Uncle André's *aversion* to arduous work is an open secret.

belittle *v.* to make something seem less important.

My feelings were hurt when the neighbors tried to *belittle* my abundant crop of tomatoes and squash.

The purpose of much campaign oratory is to *belittle* your opponent's record.

We all realized that Roger *belittled* the painting because he could not compete with the artist.

bequeath *v.* to leave money or property by a will; to pass along.

The austere, old tightwad would not *bequeath* even one penny to charity.

One of the skills I would like to *bequeath* to my children is piano playing.

Because of Allen's well-known aversion to religion, we were stunned by his plans to *bequeath* money to the church.

bizarre *adj.* strikingly odd in appearance or style; grotesque.

13

The beggar's *bizarre* street behavior alerted the police to question her.

Bizarre costumes are in order for our annual Halloween party.

I thought it rather *bizarre* for Mrs. Greene to bequeath her entire fortune to her cats.

blithe *adj.* happy and cheerful; gay.

With *blithe* disregard for our finances, Henry continued to squander his inheritance.

Lori's *blithe* attitude toward her terrible predicament was bizarre indeed.

"Hail to thee, *blithe* spirit," said the poet to the skylark.

bombastic *adj.* high-sounding; marked by use of language without much real meaning.

The citizens failed to be aroused by their mayor's *bombastic* speech.

Marc Antony's shrewd funeral address is anything but *bombastic*.

Ferris didn't get the part because the director had an aversion to his *bombastic* style.

buffoon *n.* a clown; someone who amuses with tricks and jokes.

After Bert had a few drinks, he became a willing *buffoon* at the party.

Keller was content to act the *buffoon*, but in reality he was a brilliant undercover agent.

The other players told Roger that they didn't appreciate his performance as a *buffoon*.

cache *n.* hiding place; something hidden in a hiding place.

The hungry mountain climbers gave thanks when they discovered the *cache* of canned food.

Police searched in vain for the *cache* of jewels which the thieves had skillfully concealed.

Without access to their *cache* of weapons, the terrorists were forced to surrender.

cacophony *n.* discord; harsh sound.

While we sought harmony, our enemies were pleased with *cacophony*.

14

Instead of mellow sounds, the conductor was greeted with ear-splitting *cacophony.*

The junior high band was born in *cacophony,* but their swift improvement was noted by all.

SPOTLIGHT ON

bizarre In Spanish, *bizarro* means "brave." In Italian, *bizzarro* means "angry." Somewhere those two concepts gave way to "strikingly odd in appearance," "fantastic," "grotesque" — all of which are good synonyms for *bizarre.* Remember not to confuse *bizarre* with *bazaar* which is a marketplace filled with shops.

bombastic When your language is stuffed with high-sounding words without much meaning it can be called bombastic. In Old French, *bombast* was cotton wadding. In effect, overstuffed language is bombastic. Avoid it, except when you have a special purpose in mind.

MATCHING

Match the words in Column A with their meanings in Column B.

A	B
1. autonomy	a. coercion
2. aversion	b. happy; light-hearted
3. belittle	c. pass along
4. bequeath	d. self-government
5. bizarre	e. clown
6. blithe	f. fantastic
7. bombastic	g. high-flown (language)
8. buffoon	h. clashing sounds
9. cache	i. hatred
10. cacophony	j. hiding place
	k. speak of as unimportant

FILL IN THE BLANK

Use the new words in the following sentences.

1. Despite the lengthy interrogation, the thief would not reveal the location of his _____ of jewels.

2. My fellow stockholders pleaded for greater _____ in the management of the company.

3. With a personal _____ toward smoking, Marilyn made it hard on her husband's poker cronies.

15

4. _____ threats were ignored because the general now lacked the muscle to enforce them.

5. The comedian's sour attempts to _____ the audience led to loud booing.

6. Cindy's _____ punk hairdo alienated her more conservative friends.

7. Sir John Falstaff was content to play the hard-drinking _____ in *King Henry IV*.

8. A _____ of howls came from the kennel where the terriers were housed.

9. The sight of Sonny's _____ smile could turn a dull day into a joyous one.

10. I was hoping that the widower would _____ his wife's law library to our school.

TRUE OR FALSE

Based upon the way the new words are used, identify the following sentences as True (T) or False (F).

1. Every member of the audience paid tribute to the orchestra's melodious cacophony.

2. Silas Marner's cache of gold coins was a great comfort to him.

3. At the Halloween party, the guests all wore bizarre costumes.

4. I have had an aversion toward spinach ever since I was a toddler.

5. It's poor sportsmanship to belittle the talent of the team that beats you.

LESSON 5

■ cajole ■ callous ■ capitulate ■ capricious ■ carping ■ catalyst
■ catharsis ■ caustic ■ celestial ■ censure

cajole *v.* to persuade by pleasant words or false promises.

It was Blanche's plan to *cajole* Archer into buying a bungalow at the seashore.

If anyone can *cajole* a man on a bridge from jumping, it's Sgt. Loomis.

First he tried to *cajole* the witness into testifying, then he used threats.

callous *adj.* unfeeling; insensitive.

Nurse Blatt was falsely accused of being *callous* toward her terminal patients.

It was a surprise to see the tears flowing from someone we had considered to be *callous*.

Long experience with criminals' pleas for mercy had made Judge Safian understandably *callous*.

capitulate *v.* to surrender; to cease resisting.

Colonel Leeds was adamant in his decision not to *capitulate* under any terms.

When the workers studied management's final offer, they agreed to *capitulate*.

Since the proposed terms were so ambiguous, we vowed not to *capitulate* until they were clarified.

capricious *adj.* changeable; fickle.

Our weather is so *capricious* that it's difficult to make weekend plans.

Lloyd's attorney was certain of acquittal because the charges against him were decidedly *capricious*.

Gloria's reputation for being *capricious*, for making spur-of-moment decisions, was deserved.

carping *adj.* complaining.

We were disgusted with Hillary's constant *carping* about the food.

The young recruit was advised to cease his *carping* if he wanted to survive in basic training.

Having an aversion toward politicians, Smith indulged in *carping* about the legislators' performance.

catalyst *n.* someone or something that brings about a change.

Our articulate new principal was the *catalyst* for school reform.

When a patent was granted for genetically altered mice, it was the *catalyst* for new lab research.

The rock star played the role of *catalyst* in raising funds for AIDS research.

catharsis *n.* an emotional purification or relief.

The tragedy on stage brought about a *catharsis* among the spectators.

The good news from the war zone led to a *catharsis* in the Defense Department.

Ancient Greeks felt that after a *catharsis* an individual is better able to cope with setbacks.

caustic *adj.* stinging, biting.

The comedienne played the part of a buffoon, but inwardly she suffered from the *caustic* criticism.

Caustic substances should be kept out of the reach of children.

George's *caustic* remarks were the antithesis of what we expected from such a mild-mannered gentleman.

celestial *adj.* having to do with the heavens; divine.

The new astronauts will be the *celestial* pioneers of the twenty-first century.

Every since Lydia was a youngster, she was deeply interested in *celestial* matters.

Miss America was praised lavishly for her *celestial* grace.

censure *v.* to blame; to criticize adversely. (When used as a noun, censure means "a condemnation.")

Congress agreed to *censure* the outspoken senator.

The station president will probably *censure* the TV host for his poor taste.

A vote of *censure* was taken by the faculty against the radical professor.

SPOTLIGHT ON

callous When we use this word as an adjective, we are referring to someone who is insensitive and unfeeling. Used as a noun, a callous is a part of one's skin which was exposed to pressure or friction and became hardened.

capricious The Italian word *capriccio* means "a shiver." So, if you tremble, are blown about by the wind, become changeable or fickle, you are identified as being capricious.

MATCHING

Match the words in Column A with their meanings in Column B.

	A		B
1.	cajole	a.	express disapproval of
2.	callous	b.	complaining
3.	capitulate	c.	heavenly
4.	capricious	d.	an emotional purification
5.	carping	e.	fickle
6.	catalyst	f.	agent of change
7.	catharsis	g.	surrender
8.	caustic	h.	biting; corrosive
9.	celestial	i.	unfeeling
10.	censure	j.	rigorous
		k.	coax

FILL IN THE BLANK

Use the new words in the following sentences.

1. Our visit to the planetarium was the opportunity for renewed interest in _____ matters.

2. There were occasions when _____ about the food would have been justified, but the patients refrained.

3. Everything was static in our company until a dynamic _____ for change was hired.

19

4. In a particularly _____ debate, both orators were damaged.

5. Before his angry boss could _____ him, Arnold quit.

6. It would require an articulate pleader to _____ Roberto into changing his plans.

7. When we saw the white flag, we realized they were prepared to _____.

8. It seemed to me that Samantha's selection of rental films was _____; one day she'd choose a melodramatic romance, the next day a violent gangster movie.

9. The sheriff apologized for his _____ attitude toward the attack victim.

10. The play's _____ came in Act I, much too early to be effective.

TRUE OR FALSE

Based upon the way the new words are used, identify the following sentences as T (True) or F (False).

1. Adler was entitled to praise for his callous handling of the crisis.

2. The caustic review of his acting left Greg in a fighting mood.

3. The storm was capricious and changed course constantly.

4. Vincent was cajoled into buying a raffle ticket, and he won a Mercedes.

5. Stalingrad's defenders refused to capitulate to the Germans in World War II.

REVIEW EXERCISES: LESSONS 1-5

ANALOGIES

Each question below consists of a pair of related words or phrases, followed by five lettered pairs of words or phrases. Select the lettered pair that best expresses a relationship similar to that expressed in the original pair.

1. ACQUIESCE:REBEL::
   (A) teach:professor (B) cook:diner (C) revise:editor
   (D) spread:butter (E) starve:overeater

2. ADMONISH:WARN::
   (A) pinch:touch (B) irritate:pester (C) reject:deter
   (D) scold:eulogize (E) smirk:smile

3. ALLEVIATE:PAIN::
   (A) assuage:fear (B) decorate:parade (C) refine:silo
   (D) grist:mill (E) reform:dungeon

4. ALTRUISTIC:CHARITABLE::
   (A) magnificent:unique (B) benevolent:despotic
   (C) adamant:hardheaded (D) final:tertiary
   (E) renowned:infamous

5. ARDUOUS:HERCULEAN TASK::
   (A) crowded:apartment (B) shrewd:investment
   (C) religious:rite (D) telltale:description
   (E) venomous:poison

6. AUSTERE:HARSH::
   (A) rare:common (B) secret:sinister
   (C) possible:feasible (D) innocent:sophisticated
   (E) urbane:wealthy

7. AVERSION:HATRED::
   (A) spinach:vegetable (B) transmission:car
   (C) abundance:plenty (D) willingness:loathing
   (E) hardship:endurance

8. CACOPHONY:HARMONY::
   (A) concord:flight (B) affinity:knack
   (C) honesty:candor (D) anarchy:order
   (E) laziness:indolence

9. CAJOLE:PERSUADE::
    (A) insult:deride (B) chew:swallow (C) impress:dignify
    (D) coax:quiz (E) scan:pursue

10. CATALYST:CHANGE::
    (A) mixture:result (B) architect:construction
    (C) buffoon:circus (D) cache:theft (E) agent:spy

ANTONYMS

Choose the word or phrase that is most nearly *opposite* in meaning to the word in capital letters.

1. ABSTINENCE: (A) ambivalence (B) indulgence
    (C) tardiness (D) insistence (E) tolerance

2. ACQUIESCE: (A) negotiate (B) refuse (C) coerce
    (D) intervene (E) acknowledge

3. ALIENATE: (A) transport (B) stifle
    (C) psychoanalyze (D) win over
    (E) infatuate

4. ALOOF: (A) casual (B) regional (C) rigid
    (D) marginal (E) sympathetic

5. ANTAGONISM: (A) delay (B) inundation
    (C) gratification (D) friendliness
    (E) postponement

6. ARDUOUS: (A) easy (B) benign (C) sophisticated
    (D) adamant (E) acrid

7. AUTONOMY: (A) lack of freedom (B) mobility
    (C) synchronization (D) austerity
    (E) turbulence

8. BLITHE: (A) detached (B) ignorant
    (C) melancholy (D) well-informed
    (E) shallow

9. CAUSTIC: (A) boisterous (B) mild (C) astringent
    (D) complementary (E) monastic

10. CENSURE: (A) praise (B) edit (C) authorize
    (D) inspire (E) surpervise closely

HEADLINES

Select the word which fits best in the newspaper headlines below.

1. MILLIONAIRE TO _____ FORTUNE TO HIS ALMA MATER

   (AUGMENT, BEQUEATH, ASSUAGE, ACQUIESCE)

2. JUDGE REPRIMANDED FOR _____ ATTITUDE IN COURT

   (AESTHETIC, CELESTIAL, CHARISMATIC, CAUSTIC)

3. DIRECTOR AND LEADING LADY ADMIT TO ROMANTIC

   _____

   (AFFINITY, AGGRANDIZEMENT, AMBIVALENCE, ALTRU-ISM)

4. UNION SET TO _____ AFTER UNSUCCESSFUL STRIKE

   (ARTICULATE, CAPITULATE, CAJOLE, AMELIORATE)

5. MINORITIES SEEK MORE _____ ON CAMPUS

   (AUTONOMY, AMBIGUITY, CATHARSIS, AUSTERITY)

6. _____ TREATMENT OF AIDS PATIENTS PROTESTED BY THEIR FAMILIES

   (ADAMANT, CALLOUS, ALTRUISTIC, AMENABLE)

7. MAYOR CONFUSED BY POLICE COMMISSIONER'S _____ BEHAVIOR

   (CARPING, APOCHRYPHAL, BIZARRE, ARDUOUS)

8. NEW BUILDINGS _____ HOUSING SHORTAGE

   (ALIENATE, ALLEVIATE, ATROPHY, AUGMENT)

9. ADMINISTRATION'S ATTEMPT TO _____ DEFENSE BUDGET IS DEFEATED

   (ADVOCATE, BEQUEATH, ABSTRACT, AUGMENT)

10. LAWYER CRITICIZES VERDICT AS _____

    (AESTHETIC, ALOOF, ANALOGOUS, CAPRICIOUS)

LESSON 6

■ chastise ■ chimerical ■ chronic ■ circumspect ■ clairvoyant
■ clandestine ■ clemency ■ coalesce ■ colloquial ■ commiserate

chastise *v.* to criticize severely.

If you *chastise* Jason, he immediately begins to weep.

When the caustic coach called the players together, they knew he was going to *chastise* them.

The editorial writers in our town frequently *chastise* the school board.

chimerical *adj.* absurd; wildly fanciful.

Uncle Dave was chastised by Aunt Pearl for his *chimerical* get-rich-quick schemes.

We called him callous for belittling the child's *chimerical* proposal.

Don Quixote frequently involved himself in *chimerical* flights of fancy.

chronic *adj.* lasting a long time; constant.

When Dad's cough became *chronic*, we cajoled him into getting a chest x-ray.

Janet was quickly earning a reputation as a *chronic* liar.

Our neighbor offered $500 to anyone who could cure his *chronic* hiccups.

circumspect *adj.* careful.

The lawyer struck us as aloof, but he was just being *circumspect*.

Normally *circumspect*, Rodney let slip the damaging information.

You can tell anything to Louise because she is exceptionally *circumspect*.

clairvoyant *adj.* having exceptional insight. (When clairvoyant is used as a noun, it refers to a person who has the power to see or know things that are beyond the range of natural vision.)

The *clairvoyant* housewife was occasionally used in murder cases to help discover the body.

Victor used his *clairvoyant* powers to make a fortune on Wall Street.

Cindy claimed to be *clairvoyant*, but she couldn't even find her car keys in her purse.

clandestine *adj.* secret.

Diplomats are fond of *clandestine* meetings, away from prying reporters.

The crooked food inspector had *clandestine* arrangements with several restaurant owners.

The Secretary of State served as a catalyst for the *clandestine* session between the feuding nations.

clemency *n.* mercy; mildness.

The prisoner's plea for *clemency* fell on deaf ears.

Governor Grant's policy was to personally review all Death Row *clemency* appeals.

We were delighted with the *clemency* of the Carolina winter.

coalesce *v.* to grow together; to combine.

If the competing groups could *coalesce*, they would control the election.

Allison predicted that the municipal unions would *coalesce* on their demands for a wage increase.

The two lakes *coalesced* into one.

colloquial *adj.* conversational; used in informal speech or writing.

Jeremy was chastised by his English teacher for his *colloquial* compositions.

Some political candidates find it wise to adopt a *colloquial* style of oratory.

Many words which were once considered *colloquial* have now gained respectability.

commiserate *v.* to sympathize with; to feel sorrow for another's suffering.

His teammates *commiserated* with Hank after he had struck out with the bases loaded.

While appearing to *commiserate* with Antonio, Peter was secretly happy about his neighbor's trouble.

The outpouring of those who had come to *commiserate* with her greatly warmed Rita's heart.

SPOTLIGHT ON

chimerical In Greek mythology the Chimera was a fire-breathing monster with a lion's head, a goat's body, and a serpent's tail; in short, a fanciful creature of the imagination. Knowing that, we can see why *chimerical* now means "wildly fanciful, absurd."

chronic The Greek origin of this word means "of time." You can make educated guesses about related words such as *chronicle*, *chronological*, *chronometer*, and *chronoscope*.

MATCHING

Match the words in Column A with their meanings in Column B.

A	B
1. chastise	a. mercy
2. chimerical	b. sympathize with
3. chronic	c. habitual
4. circumspect	d. seeking revenge
5. clairvoyant	e. punish
6. clandestine	f. cautious
7. clemency	g. concealed
8. coalesce	h. wildly fanciful
9. colloquial	i. conversational
10. commiserate	j. combine
	k. having insight

FILL IN THE BLANK

Use the new words in the following sentences.

1. Many inventors have been ridiculed for their seemingly _____ ideas.

2. Ever since she was a child, Dolores sensed that she possessed unusual _____ powers.

3. There were some embarrassed citizens in town when news of the heretofore _____ contract appeared in the newspaper.

4. Most Elizabethans thought that the Duke showed _____ in his treatment of Shylock.

5. "If you've come to _____, after causing the predicament we're in," Edna snarled, "we want no part of your hypocrisy."

6. Despite Albie's repeated lateness, the personnel manager did nothing more serious than _____ him.

7. Detective Anderson was assigned to the sensitive case because he had a reputation for being _____.

8. Doctor Arrowsmith's incorrect prescription managed to cure the matron's _____ condition.

9. The actor affected _____ speech but could also perform in classical roles.

10. It took four weeks of rehearsal before the ballet company could _____ and look professional.

TRUE OR FALSE

Based upon the way the new words are used, identify the following sentences as being True (T) or False (F).

1. Harry did so well at school that his parents were forced to chastise him in public.

2. It would take a circumspect police officer to tail someone as experienced as James Bond.

3. The young man who found my wallet claimed to be clairvoyant.

4. Poor Phillip was a chronic sufferer from hayfever.

5. When the prosecuting attorney promised there would be no clemency, the defendant breathed a sigh of relief.

LESSON 7

compatible *adj.* agreeing.

When the couple realized they weren't *compatible*, they sought a divorce.

On a winning team, the players and the coach are usually *compatible*.

The party powerbrokers were seeking a *compatible* vice-presidential running mate.

composure *n.* calmness.

When summoned to the principal's office, the youngster lost his *composure*.

The grief-stricken widow required tremendous *composure* to keep from breaking down at the funeral.

Casey's *composure* was remarkable considering how frightened he actually was.

conciliatory *adj.* tending to soothe or reconcile.

After a caustic debate, each contestant was seeking a *conciliatory* gesture.

Sally's *conciliatory* remarks were especially appreciated by the minority members of her council.

In a *conciliatory* frame of mind, the dictator granted clemency to his ancient enemy.

concise *adj.* saying much in few words; brief but full of meaning.

Ray has the envious reputation of being *concise* and to the point in everything he writes.

My résumé is quite *concise* because I decided to restrict it to one page.

Since Uncle Charles is usually talkative, we asked him to be *concise* for once in his life.

28

condone *v.* to forgive or overlook.

I can commiserate with you, but I find it hard to *condone* the action you took.

Her office manager was willing to *condone* Althea's poor typing, but she drew the line at chronic gum chewing.

Anton refused to *condone* the apparent child abuse in his neighbor's home.

conspicuous *adj.* clearly visible; remarkable.

With her green punk hairdo, Tina was the most *conspicuous* guest at the party.

The lieutenant advised the young detective to be circumspect, not too *conspicuous*.

Pablo Picasso was a *conspicuous* success before the age of forty.

copious *adj.* abundant.

Professor Highet gave us *copious* notes throughout his course on Dante.

The Iowa farmers luxuriated in their *copious* corn harvest.

Popcorn filled the old woman's *copious* overcoat pockets as she set out to feed the birds.

corroborate *v.* to confirm.

With only his wife to *corroborate* his alibi, Harlan was in big trouble.

Professor Ahearn's fruitless attempts to *corroborate* his colleague's findings made him suspicious.

The White House reporters checked their notebooks to *corroborate* the President's recollection.

crass *adj.* coarse; stupid.

There are many things I can forgive, but I shall never condone *crass* behavior.

The job applicant was considered *crass* for asking about vacation time.

The old-timers were incensed by the *crass* commercialism of the souvenir shops that now lined the town's main thoroughfare.

criterion *n.* standard for judging; a test.

My *criterion* for grading a meal today depends upon the amount of cholesterol it contains.

Mr. Wentworth's prime *criterion* in composition, unfortunately, is spelling.

When it comes to the purchase of an auto, our sole *criterion* is its safety record.

SPOTLIGHT ON

compatible When two people are said to be *compatible*, we mean that they get along well together. The actual Latin derivation, *compati*, is closer in meaning to "suffering together." Enough said.

concise This word implies that everything unnecessary has been left out. It comes from the Latin word *concisum* which means "cut up, cut short."

MATCHING

Match the words in Column A with their meanings in Column B.

A	B
1. compatible	a. self-control
2. composure	b. jeopardize
3. conciliatory	c. a test
4. concise	d. brief but complete
5. condone	e. support
6. conspicuous	f. overlook
7. copious	g. coarse
8. corroborate	h. easily seen
9. crass	i. abundant
10. criterion	j. in harmony
	k. tending to soothe

FILL IN THE BLANK

Use the new words in the following sentences.

1. Lefty hired a society expert to rid him of his _____ manners.

2. We were waiting to see whether the senator and his new speech writer would be a _____ team.

3. Height is no longer an acceptable _____ in the selection of urban police.

4. After being caught in a lie, George never regained his _____.

5. The seven-foot basketball player was decidedly _____ at tne party.

6. It was futile to ask the blind woman to _____ the identification of the thief.

7. My English teacher prefers crisp, _____ book reports that say a great deal within a 350-word limit.

8. The belated box of candy was Danny's _____ offering to the angry Rhonda.

9. _____ tears flowed down the child's face, starting a tiny puddle at his feet.

10. Tim was cajoled into asking Nora to _____ the unpopular action.

TRUE OR FALSE

Based upon the way the new words are used, identify the following sentences as T (True) or F (False).

1. Ham and eggs have been a compatible breakfast combination for many years.

2. Because I couldn't condone Bella's policies, I went along with them.

3. The parents' chief criterion in the selection of a principal was experience.

4. In extending his hand to the loser, the candidate made a warm, conciliatory move.

5. Seeing that the wheat crop was so copious, we knew that we would be importing once again this year.

31

LESSON 8

cryptic *adj.* secret; having a hidden meaning.

Polly's *cryptic* letter confused us as to her objectives.

F.B.I. agents asked a university expert to try to decode the *cryptic* ransom demand.

The conspicuous, *cryptic* scribbling at the tomb's entrance puzzled the archaeologists.

cursory *adj.* without attention to details.

A *cursory* glance at the difficult homework assignment was enough to destroy Marco's composure.

The parole board's *cursory* treatment of the prisoner's appeal made him pessimistic.

It requires more than *cursory* attention for me to comprehend modern poetry.

dearth *adj.* shortage.

When they spoke of a "brain drain," they were referring to the *dearth* of good physicists because of the relaxed emigration laws.

The *dearth* of citrus fruits led to a host of illnesses.

There is a current *dearth* of graduate mathematicians in the United States.

debilitate *v.* to weaken.

Some doctors will not condone sauna baths because they can *debilitate* a person.

A tropical climate can quickly *debilitate* those who are not used to it.

The cruel jailer starved his prisoners in order to *debilitate* them.

decadence *n.* decay; decline.

Many sermons tend to focus on moral *decadence* in our time.

The bestseller dealt with Western *decadence* at the close of the twentieth century.

In traveling through the neighborhood, we saw copious examples of *decadence*.

deference *n.* great respect.

Out of *deference* to my father, we never smoked in the house.

In *deference* to the famous novelist, the critics refrained from attacking his new book.

It was an act of *deference* for the police commissioner to take the mayor's side in the controversy.

deflate *v.* to let the air out of; to reduce in size or importance.

Whenever my aunt feels important, my uncle steps in to *deflate* her lofty impression of herself.

Before going on a long auto trip, I always *deflate* my tires slightly.

Seeing that Rupert was swollen with importance, we agreed to *deflate* that young man's opinion of his value to our company.

delineate *v.* to describe in words; to sketch.

When challenged to *delineate* Sam's crass behavior, we were speechless.

The great painter would merely *delineate* the outlines of the landscape, and his apprentices would fill in the details.

As the kindergarten teacher began to *delineate* Alexa's performance, the little girl's parents lost their composure.

demeanor *n.* behavior.

When the twins adopted a conciliatory tone, Sal's *demeanor* changed abruptly.

The teacher's criterion for acceptable *demeanor* was total compliance.

Unless your crass *demeanor* is reformed, we'll never be compatible.

denunciation *n.* expression of strong disapproval made openly or publicly.

The Russian premier's *denunciation* of Stalin was refreshingly unexpected.

We were astonished by the tobacco heir's *denunciation* of smoking.

When his theory couldn't be corroborated, Professor Ludwig was open to *denunciation* from his peers.

SPOTLIGHT ON

cryptic In ancient days, burial places were often hidden, sometimes below a church floor, to protect the body and its accompanying valuables from grave robbers. The Greek word *kryptos* means "hidden." Anything with a hidden meaning today can be said to be cryptic.

decadence In Latin, *cadere* means "to fall." Therefore, *decadence* refers to a "falling-off," and from there to "decline" and "decay."

MATCHING

Match the words in Column A with their meanings in Column B.

A	B
1. cryptic	a. hasty and inattentive
2. cursory	b. scarcity
3. dearth	c. to make feeble
4. debilitate	d. public condemnation
5. decadence	e. let the air out of
6. deference	f. manner
7. deflate	g. mysterious
8. delineate	h. portray
9. demeanor	i. decline
10. denunciation	j. shirk responsibility
	k. honor

FILL IN THE BLANK

Use the new words in the following sentences.

1. A police artist was asked to _____ the key features of the assailant's face.

2. The vandals planned to _____ each of the balloons in the Macy's parade.

3. Hosea's bitter _____ of his former law partner made the front pages of our papers.

4. We were unable to fathom the entertainer's _____ reference to "Mrs. Calabash."

5. Considering all of the agitating circumstances, Henrietta's calm _____ was truly remarkable.

6. Prices for the early Mickey Mantle baseball cards have skyrocketed because there is a _____ of them.

7. The _____ review of the x-rays failed to detect the tumor.

8. Although some stick-in-the-muds would disagree, wearing skimpy bathing suits is hardly a sign of cultural _____.

9. Strenuous dieting may _____ you.

10. In a gesture of _____, the French athletes rose for our national anthem.

TRUE OR FALSE

Based upon the way the new words are used, identify the following sentences as T (True) or F (False).

1. By praising Edmund lavishly, we sought to deflate his ego.

2. Although the librarian gave only cursory attention to the book, she seemed to know it intimately.

3. The show closed on Saturday because of a dearth of ticket buyers.

4. Cynthia was fond of making cryptic remarks that no one could understand.

5. Reverend Forbes hoped that the decadence of Rome would be something our society could copy.

Lesson 9

■ deprecate ■ derogatory ■ desecrate ■ despot ■ deter
■ devious ■ devoid ■ diatribe ■ didactic ■ diffuse

deprecate *v.* to express strong disapproval of.

If you continually *deprecate* Jeremy's efforts, thereby deflating his self-confidence, he may stop trying.

It was the party's custom to *deprecate* the economic policies of the incumbent.

Rather than *deprecate* my feeble attempts at writing poetry, Mr. Mazer encouraged me.

derogatory *adj.* tending to lower in estimation; degrading.

In a sharp denunciation, filled with *derogatory* criticism, the dean attacked the faculty rebels.

When Melanie apologized for her *derogatory* remarks, she displayed her maturity.

Although the *derogatory* article was published, it was softened by a thoughtful editorial.

desecrate *v.* to treat with disrespect.

The young troublemakers planned to *desecrate* the cemetery by overturning headstones.

Vietnam veterans chastised the protesters for their attempt to *desecrate* the war memorial.

The thoughtless pranksters were denounced for trying to *desecrate* our country's flag.

despot *n.* monarch with unlimited power.

My boss calls himself a benevolent *despot*, but we question the validity of that adjective.

When the kids actually delineated their father's demeanor, they realized that he was far from being a *despot*.

The *despot* inaugurated a national curfew in order to control the dissidents.

deter *v.* to discourage; to keep someone from doing something.

Nothing could *deter* Herman from achieving his ambition.

Every attempt to *deter* Cynthia only made her more determined to succeed.

They deserve acclaim for refusing to allow their handicaps to *deter* them from competing in the marathon.

devious *adj.* not straightforward; lying; roundabout.

Earl was upset because I refused to condone his *devious* ways.

Out of deference to the boy's family, the principal overlooked Vaughn's *devious* demeanor.

By following a *devious* route, we avoided the chronic gridlock.

devoid *adj.* entirely without; lacking.

The devious Kingsley was *devoid* of moral principles.

We were shipwrecked on an austere looking island, seemingly *devoid* of inhabitants.

By the time the former millionaire had reached fifty, he was completely *devoid* of asse:s.

diatribe *n.* a denunciation; bitter verbal attack.

In a lengthy *diatribe*, the governor succeeded in deprecating his predecessor's record.

The coach's *diatribe* against the umpire was a futile gesture.

After the despot's *diatribe* against foreign investors, he seized their liquid assets.

didactic *adj.* intended to instruct.

Our teacher was relentless in his affinity for *didactic* stories.

One can often communicate a *didactic* theme skillfully by sugar-coating it.

The advertising copywriter was called devious because of his concealed *didactic* message.

diffuse *adj.* spread out; wordy.

The rambling diatribe was ineffective because of its *diffuse* nature.

France's line of defense was so *diffuse* that it was easily penetrated.

Using a colloquial and *diffuse* writing style, Hunter gave his editor apoplexy.

SPOTLIGHT ON

despot A Greek youngster might have been apprenticed to a *despotes*, the word for "master." Someone who has complete control over you and exercises tyrranical authority is a despot.In the case of a ruler who is compassionate rather than cruel, we refer to the ruler as a benevolent despot.

diatribe The Greek origin of this word means "a waste of time." Many a diatribe, when it goes unheeded by the subject of the denunciation, is probably a waste of time.

MATCHING

Match the words in Column A with their meanings in Column B.

A	B
1. deprecate	a. absolute ruler
2. derogatory	b. roundabout
3. desecrate	c. teacherlike
4. despot	d. empty
5. deter	e. degrading
6. devious	f. to disregard the sacredness of
7. devoid	g. to express strong disapproval of
8. diatribe	h. desperately in need of
9. didactic	i. bitter verbal attack
10. diffuse	j. to discourage
	k. spread out

FILL IN THE BLANK

Use the new words in the following sentences.

1. When his army deserted him, the _____ was forced to flee for his life.

2. The sermon was filled with _____ anecdotes that bored the congregation.

3. Desmond was used to having his older brother _____ his chimerical suggestions.

4. Elaine's reputation for being _____ made it difficult for us to accept her explanation.

5. No obstacle can _____ a determined person from reaching an achievable objective.

6. After the threat to _____ Michelangelo's statue, a guard was stationed in front of it.

7. Sticks and stones may break my bones but _____ remarks will never harm me.

8. The young playwright had the kernel of a good idea, but his plot was too _____ to be effective.

9. Jurors found the prosecutor's closing argument to be _____ of merit.

10. It was amusing to hear my doctor's _____ against nicotine and later to see him light up a cigar.

TRUE OR FALSE

Based upon the way the new words are used, identify the following sentences as T (True) or F (False).

1. The family of the deposed ruler vowed not to allow anyone to desecrate his name.

2. Herman was told that his essay would have had greater impact if it hadn't been so clearly didactic.

3. Fast food meals are often filled with calories but devoid of good nutrition.

4. Some devious people are convinced that they can outwit a lie detector test.

5. Mom always felt that if you had only derogatory statements to make about a person, you were better off keeping quiet.

LESSON 10

■ diminution ■ discerning ■ disdain ■ dismantle ■ disparage
■ disparity ■ disperse ■ disposition ■ dissipated ■ distraught

diminution *n.* a lessening.

The *diminution* in nightly air raids was welcomed by the Londoners.

After we had rapped on the ceiling, there was a perceptible *diminution* in noise from upstairs.

Out of deference to the inventor of the catalytic converter, the government admitted there had been a *diminution* in the pollution.

discerning *adj.* keenly perceptive; shrewd. (When the related verb form *discern* is used, it means "to perceive; to recognize as distinct or different; to see things clearly.")

When it came to selecting the correct investments, Paul was quite *discerning*.

The *discerning* movie review pointed out the serious weaknesses in the film.

In a *discerning* analysis of his opponent's platform, the candidate revealed his intellectual superiority.

disdain *n.* a feeling of contempt for anything that is regarded as unworthy; scorn.

Jefferson High held Collier Tech's team in *disdain*.

Having nothing but *disdain* for his rival, it was easy to deprecate the man's ability.

With cold *disdain* the atheist proceeded to desecrate the holy image.

dismantle *v.* to pull down; to take apart.

Before the movers could take the pool table out, they had to *dismantle* it.

The owner decided to *dismantle* the team before capitulating to the union.

Exterminators practically had to *dismantle* the chimney before cajoling the raccoon into leaving.

disparage *v.* to discredit; to belittle.

In bizarre fashion, Norma went out of her way to *disparage* everything her sister did.

Evans quickly learned that it was folly to *disparage* his employer's proposals.

Warren was devious enough to *disparage* Bobby's work while seeming to praise it.

disparity *n.* lack of equality; difference.

Birth certificates corroborated the wide *disparity* in the couple's ages.

Because our players are devoid of any height, there is a considerable *disparity* between both teams.

The *disparity* between the skills of the two chess players made for an uneven contest.

disperse *v.* to send off in different directions.

When the tear gas is hurled, the crowd will *disperse*.

I waited for the reporters to *disperse*, then approached the senator with complete composure.

After the U.N. session, the delegates will *disperse* to all corners of the globe.

disposition *n.* nature; tendency.

The melancholy foreman had disdain for any worker with a cheery *disposition*.

My dilatory *disposition* got me into trouble with many professors.

Rico's optimistic *disposition* was the antithesis of Monte's pessimistic nature.

dissipated *adj.* indulging excessively in sensual pleasures. (The related verb *dissipate* means "to spend or use wastefully or extravagantly; to scatter in various directions.")

As the weeks went by, the portrait slowly took on a *dissipated* look, while the model's face remained cryptically youthful.

The legislator was disparaged in the press after the news of his *dissipated* lifestyle leaked out.

Count Igor *dissipated* his family's fortune on polo ponies and speedboats.

distraught *adj.* in a state of mental conflict and confusion; distracted.

Ophelia's *distraught* brother flung himself into her grave and uttered a bombastic challenge to Hamlet.

The bishop tried to commiserate with the parents, but they were too *distraught* to be consoled.

News of the plane's explosion brought many *distraught* relatives to the airport.

SPOTLIGHT ON

disparage If a medieval nobleman were to be compared to a peasant, he would consider himself matched unequally. "To match unequally" is the meaning of the French verb *desparagier*. Hence, our word *disparage*, which means "to lower one's reputation" or "to belittle someone."

dissipated One of the meanings of this word is "to indulge excessively in sensual or foolish pleasures." It comes from a Latin word which meant "scattered" or "spread in different directions." When we describe people as dissipated, in effect we are saying that they have scattered or wasted their resources.

MATCHING

Match the words in Column A with their meanings in Column B.

A	B
1. diminution	a. contempt
2. discerning	b. astute
3. disdain	c. scatter
4. dismantle	d. difference
5. disparage	e. sharply critical
6. disparity	f. spent wastefully
7. disperse	g. lower the reputation of
8. disposition	h. distracted
9. dissipated	i. take apart
10. distraught	j. temperament
	k. decrease

FILL IN THE BLANK

Use the new words in the following sentences.

1. Because she was considered the most _____ member of the firm, she was assigned the most difficult cases.

2. The _____ in first quarter earnings led to a sharp drop in the value of the company's stock.

3. When the marks of the difficult exam were posted, there were several _____ seniors crying in front of the bulletin board.

4. We noted a marked _____ between what Uncle Manny said and what he actually did.

5. Grace will invariably leave a ten-cent tip to any waiter who treats her with _____.

6. After a one-month furlough, the private returned to camp with a shockingly _____ appearance.

7. It goes against my _____ to hold a grudge.

8. Additional police were summoned when the demonstrators refused to _____.

9. Far be it for me to _____ anyone's attempt to bring low-cost housing to our city.

10. I wouldn't allow the negative forces to _____ our school's great reputation.

TRUE OR FALSE

Based upon the way the new words are used, identify the following sentences as T (True) or F (False).

1. The surgeon's good news made us all distraught.

2. With a diminution in his chest pains, Irwin decided to reduce his medication.

3. Sales managers prefer hiring people who have pleasant dispositions.

4. The disparity between both signatures was so slight that the forgery went undetected.

5. When Kimberly's novel was disparaged by the critics, she was thrilled.

43

REVIEW EXERCISES: LESSONS 6-10

ANALOGIES

Each question below consists of a pair of related words or phrases, followed by five lettered pairs of words or phrases. Select the lettered pair that best expresses a relationship similar to that in the original pair.

1. DISPOSITION:EVIL::
   (A) face:wrinkled (B) publication:bargain
   (C) tennis:serious (D) robot:communicative
   (E) catcall:unpleasant

2. DISPARITY:INEQUALITY::
   (A) talent:exposure (B) safety:net
   (C) flattery:compliment (D) luck:prayer
   (E) scythe:farmer

3. DIATRIBE:SPEECH::
   (A) allergy:pollen (B) response:fable
   (C) magnolia:tree (D) command:warning
   (E) lightning:nature

4. DESPOT:POPULACE::
   (A) teacher:parents (B) editor:publisher
   (C) meteorologist:rain (D) carton:books
   (E) monarch:citizenry

5. DIMINUTION:EXPANSION::
   (A) disease:treatment (B) typing: communication
   (C) calm:anger (D) calories:exercise
   (E) theatre:drama

6. DISDAIN:ADMIRATION::
   (A) stubbornness:flexibility
   (B) heat:dampness (C) vim:vigor
   (D) inspiration:sermon (E) sorrow:melancholy

7. CLEMENCY:HARSHNESS::
   (A) flower:tulip (B) building:skyscraper
   (C) age:beauty (D) grand jury:justice
   (E) stallion:mare

8. COMPOSURE:PANIC::
   (A) sympathy:indifference (B) religion:freedom
   (C) intelligence:forthrightness (D) unhappiness:protest
   (E) disposition:moodiness

9. CRITERION:STANDARD::
   (A) winter:fur coat (B) verdict:decision
   (C) hospital:volunteer (D) signal:bulb
   (E) bucket:coal

10. CLANDESTINE:MEETING::
    (A) boring:essay (B) shrewd:ambition
    (C) tropical:coat (D) ornamental:gathering
    (E) clearance:sale

ANTONYMS

Choose the word or phrase that is most nearly *opposite* in meaning to the word in capital letters.

1. CHIMERICAL: (A) watchful (B) logical (C) antagonistic
   (D) blazing (E) unassuming

2. CIRCUMSPECT: (A) precious (B) confined (C) portly
   (D) careless (E) blind

3. CONSPICUOUS: (A) invisible (B) tolerant (C) rude
   (D) talented (E) suspicious

4. COPIOUS: (A) bulky (B) disparaging
   (C) willing to make peace (D) regrettable
   (E) inadequate

5. CURSORY: (A) in depth (B) sensitive (C) apologetic
   (D) inclined to humor (E) portable

6. DEBILITATE: (A) forgive (B) strengthen
   (C) make irritable (D) add to (E) withhold

7. DEVIOUS: (A) accessible (B) troublesome
   (C) straightforward (D) merciful
   (E) willing to forgive

8. DIFFUSE: (A) concentrated (B) marginal
   (C) imperfect (D) silent (E) intellectual

9. DIMINUTION: (A) interruption (B) contradiction
   (C) increase (D) rejection (E) acceptance

10. DISMANTLE: (A) pollute (B) confirm (C) oversee
    (D) ignore (E) erect

HEADLINES

Select the word that fits best in the newspaper headlines below.

1. LAWYER SEEKS _____ FOR WAR VETERAN CLIENT
   (COMPOSURE, DEFERENCE, CLEMENCY, DISPARITY)

2. STATION MANAGER TO _____ DISC JOCKEY FOR POOR TASTE
   (CONDONE, DESECRATE, DEBILITATE, CHASTISE)

3. THE HOMELESS _____ AFTER RAID ON RAILROAD STATION WAITING ROOM
   (DISPERSE, DEPRECATE, CORROBORATE, DISMANTLE)

4. WE LIVE IN A TIME OF _____, SOCIOLOGIST LAMENTS
   (DENUNCIATION, COMPOSURE, DECADENCE, CLAIRVOYANCE)

5. CITY COUNCIL ATTACKED OVER _____ BUDGET DEFICIT
   (DIDACTIC, CHRONIC, COLLOQUIAL, ELUSIVE)

6. _____ IN ACID RAIN CHEERS OUR NORTHERN NEIGHBORS
   (DISPARITY, DIATRIBE, DIMINUTION, DISPOSITION)

7. MOTHER _____ OVER COURT DECISION TO TAKE HER CHILDREN AWAY
   (DISSIPATED, DEVOID, CLANDESTINE, DISTRAUGHT)

8. SEEK EYEWITNESSES TO _____ IDENTIFICATION OF JEWEL THIEF
   (DISMANTLE, CORROBORATE, DESECRATE, COALESCE)

9. NO LONGER _____, SAY FORMER LOVEBIRDS
   (COMPATIBLE, CHIMERICAL, CIRCUMSPECT, DEROGATORY)

10. PERSONNEL MANAGER ASKED TO _____ NEW JOB RESPONSIBILITIES
    (DELINEATE, DEFLATE, DISPERSE, CONDONE)

LESSON 11

dogmatic *adj.* positive and emphatic in asserting opinions.

Randy's huge ego makes all of his pronouncements sound *dogmatic.*

Our organization's secretary, a former college instructor, has an affinity for being *dogmatic.*

We would have accepted Lavinia's statement had it been less *dogmatic.*

dormant *adj.* lying asleep; in a state of rest.

Dormant for five years, the soprano's voice had lost none of its tonal clarity.

The reform movement in our conservative town has been *dormant* for over a decade.

Due to illegal dumping of toxic wastes, pollution of our rivers is no longer a *dormant* issue.

duplicity *n.* deceitfulness.

The guilty accountant's *duplicity* was discovered in a random audit.

When cheating a cheater, Troy doesn't hesitate to use his own *duplicity.*

The director of the lottery was arrested after his *duplicity* was uncovered.

ebb *v.* to decline.

Investors watched their fortunes *ebb* as the stock market plunged to a new low.

Samson felt his strength *ebb* as his curly locks were snipped off.

Ebb tide is expected at 7:30 p.m.

eclectic *adj.* consisting of selections from various sources.

Hardy's *eclectic* taste in art made his home into a conversation piece.

With an *eclectic* interest in books, Sheila collected everything from Shakespeare to Superman.

My fixation with baseball has ebbed, and now I'm a more *eclectic* sports fan.

efface *v.* to wipe out; to erase.

My school's custodian makes a daily attempt to *efface* the ugly graffiti.

If I could *efface* the errors of my youth, the old man wondered, would I do it?

A devious attempt to *efface* the signature didn't fool the bank teller.

effervescent *adj.* lively; giving off bubbles.

Señorita Flores is admired for her blithe sense of humor and *effervescent* personality.

Roberta was often described as *effervescent*, but that spirit is dormant these days.

Because I do not enjoy carbonated drinks, I do not like the *effervescent* quality of ginger ale.

egregious *adj.* extraordinarily bad.

An *egregious* bookkeeping error cost our company $1,000,000.

Small errors could be overlooked, but there was no way to condone Jerry's *egregious* mistake.

We were unable to efface the *egregious* libel before the newspaper went to press.

elucidate *v.* to make clear.

Public relations experts were hired to *elucidate* the chairman's position.

Only a freshman would have the effrontery to offer to *elucidate* the professor's theory.

The new tax reform is so complicated that a guide sheet is required to *elucidate* its provisions.

elusive *adj.* hard to grasp; baffling.

The philospher's main point was so *elusive* that we never did fully comprehend it.

Despite the efforts of an entire team of anthropologists, the clues remained *elusive*.

It took all of Sherlock Holmes's skill to capture the *elusive* criminal.

SPOTLIGHT ON

efface While this verb means "to rub out," it does have a secondary meaning: "to make inconspicuous." That harks back to the French origin, *effacer*, which means "face away." A self-effacing person prefers to be out of the spotlight.

effervescent The lively person at a party who bubbles over with energy is called effervescent. Tracing it back to its Latin origin, we note that *fervescere* means "to begin to boil."

MATCHING

Match the words in Column A with their meanings in Column B.

<u>A</u>	<u>B</u>
1. dogmatic	a. selecting from different sources
2. dormant	b. inactive
3. duplicity	c. baffling
4. ebb	d. grow weaker
5. eclectic	e. emphatic in asserting opinions
6. efface	f. explain
7. effervescent	g. outstanding for bad reasons
8. egregious	h. bubbling
9. elucidate	i. humble
10. elusive	j. erase
	k. double-dealing

FILL IN THE BLANK

Use the new words in the following sentences.

1. When it comes to restaurants we're quite _____ and willing to experiment.

2. The articulate press agent jumped at the chance to _____ his ideas for publicizing the concert.

3. Although Herbert was a law-abiding citizen, his early reputation for _____ was hard to get rid of.

4. The Bay of Pigs invasion of Cuba turned out to be an _____ disaster.

5. Hope for an early rescue of the infant in the well began to _____ as darkness set in.

6. Using computers, Harvard mathematicians were finally able to discover the _____ factors and solve the equation.

7. The City Council voted to _____ the radical's name from the war memorial.

8. I have an aversion to people who are so _____ that they refuse to listen to a contrary opinion.

9. Benjy's hope for training another champ lay _____ until Lefty came along.

10. Rosa's _____ personality made her a perfect choice for head cheerleader.

TRUE OR FALSE

Based upon the way the new words are used, identify the following sentences as T (True) or F (False).

1. Dogmatic people tend to be intolerant of the views of others.

2. The poet's effervescent responses were in keeping with her shy, withdrawn demeanor.

3. As we approach 5 p.m. each day, Farrell's vitality begins to ebb.

4. After an unannounced visit by the auditors, the bank teller's duplicity was uncovered.

5. The virus was dormant for some years but has now appeared in a life threatening form.

LESSON 12

■ embellish ■ embroil ■ emulate ■ enervate ■ engender
■ enhance ■ enigma ■ ephemeral ■ equanimity ■ equivocate

embellish *v.* to decorate; to elaborate upon.

Our effervescent principal can be relied upon to *embellish* his graduation message with a few spirited anecdotes.

For $5000, the decorator promised to *embellish* our living room with continental touches.

If you encourage the state trooper, he'll *embellish* the tale of how he uncovered the cache of the bank robbers.

embroil *v.* to involve in a quarrel.

The rival party sought a way to *embroil* the government in a dispute over the economy.

Umpires are loath to *embroil* themselves in controversies between opposing managers.

It was the devious lawyer's plan to *embroil* the plaintiff in a series of noisy disagreements.

emulate *v.* to try to equal or surpass.

When they were in high school, Dudley's kid brother always tried to *emulate* him.

In qualifying for the medal, you will *emulate* your sister's performance.

We hired a Japanese efficiency expert to *emulate* his foreign success in our factory.

enervate *v.* to weaken, to lessen the strength of.

Ali would *enervate* his opponents by allowing them to punch themselves into weariness.

Our battalion was so fit that not even a ten-mile forced march could *enervate* us.

Strenuous dieting will *enervate* most people.

51

engender *v.* to cause, produce, bring into being.

Those sneaky actions are sure to *engender* suspicion.

Our aggression will *engender* a swift response from the enemy.

When you introduce a new product, you are certain to *engender* competition.

enhance *v.* to add to; to make greater in value.

The staff development program was designed to *enhance* the skills of the company's executives.

One way to *enhance* the value of a good painting is to frame it aesthetically.

Lindsay discovered that a sure way to *enhance* her position in the law firm was to win a difficult case for a wealthy client.

enigma *n.* a puzzle; a baffling situation.

Why a bright student should make such egregious errors is an *enigma*.

If I could solve the *enigma* of my sensible brother's recently bizarre behavior, I'd be a genius.

Oedipus passed the test by unravelling the *enigma* which the Sphinx had posed.

ephemeral *adj.* lasting for only a short time.

Newspapers may be regarded as *ephemeral* publications whereas books have greater permanence.

In Hollywood, where you are only as good as your last picture, reputations tend to be *ephemeral.*

With an *ephemeral* interest in so many areas, Richie easily succumbed to boredom.

equanimity *n.* evenness of temper.

Facing every crisis with *equanimity*, the authoritarian president inspired confidence among the people.

I admire the way Charlotte retains her *equanimity* and composure amidst the excitement of the stock exchange.

A good test of comedians is to observe their display of *equanimity* when hecklers are making derogatory remarks.

equivocate *v.* to use double meanings in order to mislead; to be shifty; to quibble.

> One candidate is honest and blunt; the other prefers to *equivocate* on controversial issues.

> Watching the forthright decision maker suddenly *equivocate* presented me with an enigma.

> If you choose to *equivocate*, you may ultimately lose the support of both parties who are embroiled in the dispute.

SPOTLIGHT ON

enervate "To take away from the sinews or nerves" is the original meaning of this word. Currently, we use enervate when we mean "to lessen the strength of."

enigma As we know from Oedipus and other Greek legends, they were fond of riddles. The Greek word *ainigma* means "to speak in riddles" and is the origin of enigma.

MATCHING

Match the words in Column A with their meanings in Column B.

<u>A</u>	<u>B</u>
1. embellish	a. involve in a quarrel
2. embroil	b. add beauty to
3. emulate	c. theoretical
4. enervate	d. to cause
5. engender	e. heighten
6. enhance	f. a riddle
7. enigma	g. to be ambiguous
8. ephemeral	h. debilitate
9. equanimity	i. very short-lived
10. equivocate	j. calmness
	k. to try to equal

FILL IN THE BLANK

Use the new words in the following sentences.

1. When Darnley began to _____ we knew he couldn't be trusted.

2. Mr. Micawber, ever the optimist, took his setbacks with great _____.

3. Believing that life was _____, the young couple determined to live it to its fullest.

4. It's a cliché to assert that a fisherman will _____ the tale of his latest catch.

5. By reading the ghost story aloud at midnight, I hoped to _____ an air of excitement among the guests.

6. The many Rambo sequels were attempts to _____ the original's success.

7. A certain way to _____ my father in an argument was to mention the welfare state.

8. How we could lose the championship to such an inferior team remains an _____ to this day.

9. Carol Sue was determined to _____ her reputation in the Foreign Service by learning to speak Chinese.

10. One hour in a sauna bath will _____ the most active person.

TRUE OR FALSE

Based upon the way the new words are used, identify the following sentences as T (True) or F (False).

1. Following sixteen straight hours on the job, I was totally enervated.

2. Randy likes to equivocate, letting us know exactly how he feels on every subject.

3. Embroiled in a barroom fight, the scrappy Clancy was at his happiest.

4. By preparing an attractive résumé, you can enhance your opportunities for being hired.

5. The novel had an ephemeral reign on the bestseller list, lasting only one week.

LESSON 13

esoteric *adj.* understood by only a select few.

Dr. Thorpe's scholarship was so *esoteric* that it attracted little attention.

I avoid books with *esoteric* themes, but enjoy those which are realistic and easy to comprehend.

The disc jockey's patter had become so *esoteric* that it led to a dearth of listeners.

eulogy *n.* high praise for a deceased person.

When Reverend Foster delivered the *eulogy*, he embellished it with a few apochryphal stories.

The distraught family members were comforted greatly by the moving *eulogy*.

The young student was very honored when he was asked to deliver the *eulogy* for his favorite professor.

euphemism *n.* use of an indirect expression in place of one that is harsh.

Since I didn't want to hurt Debby's feelings, I searched for an appropriate *euphemism*.

Ted has an aversion to *euphemism*, preferring to speak directly and not pull his punches.

Referring to the elevator operator as a transportation controller is a *euphemism* that we consider to be ridiculous.

evanescent *adj.* gradually disappearing; fleeting.

Max's unconcern was apparent as he showed only an *evanescent* interest in the new project.

The *evanescent* student protest ebbed as soon as the cafeteria food improved.

Unfortunately, Holly's good resolutions were frequently *evanescent*.

55

exacerbate *v.* to make a situation worse; to irritate.

One way to *exacerbate* their feelings of anger is to trivialize the quarrel.

Millicent's seemingly innocent proposal may actually *exacerbate* the problem.

If you want to *exacerbate* your upset stomach, try the spicy chili.

exemplary *adj.* serving as a model.

Matthew Alexander's stature was enhanced by the report of his *exemplary* conduct in nursery school.

A chestful of medals were presented to General MacArthur following his *exemplary* performance in combat.

We pay Marjorie well because she's an *exemplary* babysitter.

expedient *adj.* useful; advantageous; based on self-interest. (When *expedient* is used as a noun, it is "a means of bringing about a desired result.")

Henry's decisions are never *expedient* ones because he is genuinely altruistic.

Hiring a part-time secretary was an *expedient* move which paid off.

We formed a car pool ten years ago as an evanescent *expedient*, but it's still operational.

expedite *v.* to make easy and quick; to speed up.

In order to *expedite* matters we hired three additional workers.

By purchasing a postage meter, Harvey was able to *expedite* the shipment of our mail.

When my mother is preparing our favorite dishes, we like to come into the kitchen to help *expedite* the meal.

expunge *v.* to erase; to remove completely.

Miss Porter promised to *expunge* the bad conduct notation from Danielle's report card if she improved conspicuously.

The jurors were directed to *expunge* the derogatory remarks from their memory.

For twelve years, Sergeant Phillips petitioned the army to *expunge* the court martial from his record.

extol *v.* to praise highly.

It's my intention to *extol* Bonnie's successful fund-raising efforts at our next club meeting.

In his eulogy, Marc Antony said that he came to bury Caesar, not to *extol* him.

You may wish to *extol* Adrienne for her human relations skills in order to counteract the diatribe launched against her.

SPOTLIGHT ON

euphemism When a butcher refers to himself as a "meat coordinator," we say that he is using a euphemism, or mild or indirect expression. The Greek origin of this word means "to speak with fair words."

expedite *Ex* means "out" and *pedan* is the Latin word for "foot." When you remove your foot from an entanglement, you help to expedite matters.

MATCHING

Match the words in Column A with their meanings in Column B.

A	B
1. esoteric	a. a less offensive term
2. eulogy	b. to aggravate a situation
3. euphemism	c. advantageous
4. evanescent	d. vanishing
5. exacerbate	e. blot out
6. exemplary	f. worth imitating
7. expedient	g. speed up
8. expedite	h. understood only by a select few
9. expunge	i. commend
10. extol	j. peruse carefully
	k. high praise for a deceased person

FILL IN THE BLANK

Use the new words in the following sentences.

1. In an _____ move, two dozen machinists were laid off at our factory.

2. It would be well, the therapist felt, if Marvin could _____ the incident from his memory.

3. Since Alvin knew that they were going to _____ him to the heavens, he stayed away from the ceremony.

4. A plain cook, Molly had no time for _____ recipes.

5. Andy Warhol, speaking of the _____ quality of fame, said that each of us was entitled to only fifteen lifetime minutes in the spotlight.

6. When we thought that the argument had been resolved, along came Smith to _____ it.

7. The minister discarded his prepared _____ and spoke off-the-cuff.

8. My teacher said it was an _____ job of typing but a poor sample of creative writing.

9 You can _____ things by filling out the application before your interview.

10. Referring to the undertaker as a "bereavement counsellor" was a classical _____.

TRUE OR FALSE

Based upon the way the new words are used, identify the following sentences as T (True) or F (False).

1. The drilling in the street exacerbated my nervous condition.

2. Courtney's eulogy was so moving that he was asked to deliver two more funeral orations within the same month.

3. Muttering some esoteric mumbo-jumbo, the fortune teller pretended to be in touch with the spirit world.

4. I find it hard sometimes to say the word "died" and am more comfortable with the euphemism "passed away."

5. We used a black lettering pen to expunge the words so that everyone could see them.

LESSON 14

■ facilitate ■ fallacy ■ fastidious ■ fervor ■ fitful ■ flagrant
■ fledgling ■ forlorn ■ formidable ■ fortuitous

facilitate *v.* to make easy; to help bring about.

The exemplary guidance given us by the bank helped to *facilitate* the merger.

In order to *facilitate* the sale, I cajoled Lorraine into signing a blank check.

To *facilitate* our move, the company sent a crew to crate all of the furniture.

fallacy *n.* false idea; mistaken belief.

By the time I discovered the *fallacy* in his argument, he had already claimed victory.

The economist revealed the *fallacy* in the govenment's proposal.

We showed the *fallacy* in the public belief that our opponents were invulnerable.

fastidious *adj.* hard to please; dainty in taste.

Lauren was so particular about her home that she was extolled as a *fastidious* housekeeper.

In *The Odd Couple*, Jack Lemmon was the *fastidious* one, while the sloppy Walter Matthau was his antithesis.

Everett was so *fastidious* that his messy fraternity brothers refused to room with him.

fervor *n.* intense emotion; great warmth of feeling.

Alicia does her volunteer work with tremendous *fervor*.

Our initial *fervor* subsided when the public failed to support us.

The *fervor* of our Olympic relay team was etched onto every runner's face.

fitful *adj.* spasmodic; intermittent.

Monte's *fitful* sleep tended to exacerbate his normal irritability.

"After life's *fitful* fever," Macbeth said, "the king is finally at rest."

When the *fitful* machine gun fire increased in tempo, the government troops dispersed.

flagrant *adj.* outrageous; glaringly offensive.

Citing extenuating circumstances, Peter asked his boss to overlook the *flagrant* bookkeeping error.

After having been accused of a *flagrant* misuse of company assets, the treasurer resigned.

Drinking from one's saucer is considered a *flagrant* breach of etiquette.

fledgling *adj.* newly developed; little known. (When *fledgling* is used as a noun, it refers to a young bird or an inexperienced person.)

Although their *fledgling* soda business is only a year old, the two women have been offered $3,000,000 for it.

Luckily, the *fledgling* pilot's egregious blunder was discovered before the plane departed.

The *fledgling*, suddenly an orphan, had to find its own food.

forlorn *adj.* deserted; left alone and neglected; unhappy.

When the TV camera showed the *forlorn* youngster at the graveside, there wasn't a dry eye in the viewing audience.

Feeling *forlorn* and full of self-pity, Eddie was a danger to himself.

Old pictures of Ellis Island immigrants are ambivalent in that they portray happy faces as well as *forlorn* ones.

formidable *adj.* hard to overcome; to be dreaded.

The champion made a silly reference to his opponent, showing that he underestimated that *formidable* rival.

Requirements for some of the Ivy League schools were so *formidable* that Laurie became distraught over her chances.

Seemingly a mild-mannered reporter, Clark Kent was actually the *formidable* Superman.

fortuitous *adj.* happening by chance.

Wally's *fortuitous* meeting with Mr. Berman in the restaurant helped to facilitate the agreement between both their companies.

My *fortuitous* discovery of the cache of valuable stamps enabled me to buy a motorcycle.

With one *fortuitous* question, the reporter unravelled the actor's composure.

SPOTLIGHT ON

fastidious   Interestingly enough, this word's noun form in Latin means "loathing." Someone who showed displeasure when things were not right, who was easily disgusted, is now called *fastidious* or "hard to please."

flagrant   To commit a *flagrant* error is to make an outrageous blunder. Flagrant, however, originally was used to mean "burning" or "blazing." Anything as attention-getting as a fire became glaringly offensive or notorious because flagrant now has that connotation.

MATCHING

Match the words in Column A with their meanings in Column B.

A	B
1. facilitate	a. false idea
2. fallacy	b. irregular
3. fastidious	c. humble
4. fervor	d. assist
5. fitful	e. newly-developed
6. flagrant	f. hard to overcome
7. fledgling	g. intense emotion
8. forlorn	h. notorious
9. formidable	i. accidental
10. fortuitous	j. hard to please
	k. abandoned

FILL IN THE BLANK

Use the new words in the following sentences.

1. The senator's fund-raising ability will make him a _____ candidate for re-election.

2. Physicists continue to search for a _____ in Einstein's theory.

3. Because his accessories were always color-coordinated, Dominick was known as a _____ dresser.

4. The emotionless candidate lacked _____, his supporters complained.

5. The showers, an off-and-on nuisance all day, could best be described as _____.

6. I offered my last-ditch proposal in the hope that it might _____ a reconciliation.

7. The SUPERCENTER, a _____ training program for administrators, is only in its first year of operation.

8. As a result of the completely _____ encounter with a movie producer, Donna Mae was offered a screen test.

9. The lone sheep in the meadow looked so _____ that it evoked our sympathy.

10. A _____ oversight by the ground controller almost led to a mid-air disaster.

TRUE OR FALSE

Based upon the way the new words are used, identify the following sentences as T (True) or F (False).

1. Debra was so fastidious about her appearance that she always appeared at her best.

2. Although Spud was only 5'6", he was so talented that the other teams regarded him as a formidable foe.

3. Cheating at the school was flagrant, forcing the administration to take punitive action.

4. Bumping into Diana on the train was a fortuitous circumstance for which Lionel was most grateful.

5. Since he was quite shy, the company's chief executive scheduled press conferences only fitfully.

LESSON 15

■ furtive ■ galvanize ■ garbled ■ garner ■ garrulous ■ gratuitous
■ guile ■ gullible ■ hackneyed ■ haphazard

furtive *adj.* done quickly and with stealth to avoid being noticed; secret

With a *furtive* glance over his shoulder, the forlorn shopkeeper locked the store and stole away into the night.

Cynthia's *furtive* gesture and cryptic remark did not go unnoticed.

Long experience with British Intelligence had given Col. Forsythe the *furtive* manners of a pickpocket.

galvanize *v.* to arouse suddenly; to startle.

The senator hoped that his formidable rival's strength in the polls would *galvanize* his own supporters into action.

It took a nuclear mishap at Chernobyl to *galvanize* the peace movement into protesting vigorously.

The fortuitous meeting did more to *galvanize* Edna into decorating her house than all of her husband's subtle hints were able to accomplish.

garbled *adj.* confused; mixed up (e.g., facts, statements, letters).

The *garbled* message failed to facilitate the ambulance's arrival.

Morton's testimony was so *garbled* that the judge ordered it stricken from the record.

After having been hit on the head, the normally articulate woman's words were badly *garbled*.

garner *v.* to gather and store away; to collect.

By paying close attention, you may be able to *garner* some information which will elucidate the situation.

From all that Michelle could *garner* furtively, there was a wide disparity between the truth and the official explanation.

Vinny's hobby was to *garner* bits of incriminating evidence and to keep them salted away as his insurance policy.

garrulous *adj.* talkative.

The *garrulous* baseball manager embellished his anecdotes, providing colorful copy for the sports reporters.

We were faced with an enigma when the heretofore *garrulous* witness suddenly took the Fifth Amendment.

Nothing galvanizes me into leaving a beauty parlor as much as a *garrulous* hairdresser.

gratuitous *adj.* freely given; unnecessary; uncalled-for.

My boss concluded an otherwise exemplary speech with a *gratuitous* slur which ruined the rest of the evening.

Hillary's *gratuitous* suggestion was rejected by the other guests who blithely ignored it.

Seated at the rear of the room, Victor was nervy enough to heckle the performers with *gratuitous* insults.

guile *n.* crafty deceit; cunning.

Many clever figures from Greek mythology relied upon *guile* as an expedient.

My aversion to the *guile* which Elton used exacerbated our shaky relationship.

Iago's *guile* and duplicity were successful in destroying Othello.

gullible *adj.* easily deceived.

The con man told a flagrant lie but the *gullible* investors swallowed it.

Despite the solid evidence that was presented, Bobby was still *gullible* enough to believe in flying saucers.

People who are naive and *gullible* are at the mercy of clever swindlers.

hackneyed *adj.* used too often; trite; commonplace.

Creative writers cringe when they hear egregiously *hackneyed* expressions.

Ralph's eulogy was effective although it was filled with *hackneyed* tributes to the deceased gentleman.

While my composition was technically correct, my teacher chastised me, pointing out its many *hackneyed* descriptions.

haphazard *adj.* not planned; random.

Because of a *haphazard* selection, the least qualified applicant was chosen.

Taking *haphazard* aim, the hunter committed a fatal error.

Shirley's *haphazard* denunciation alienated the dinner guests.

SPOTLIGHT ON

furtive The Latin nouns *fur* and *furtum* mean "theft" and "thief." People who move in a furtive manner may be law-abiding, but there is a tendency to assume that their intentions are not honorable.

haphazard Whereas many of the words in this book may be traced back to Latin origins, this one has Scandinavian and French parentage. The Scandinavian word *happ* means "chance," "luck," and the French *hasard* means "a game of dice." To take a chance on the roll of the dice is to operate haphazardly.

MATCHING

Match the words in Column A with their meanings in Column B.

A	B
1. furtive	a. confused
2. galvanize	b. talkative
3. garbled	c. sluggish; apathetic
4. garner	d. collect
5. garrulous	e. arouse
6. gratuitous	f. used too often
7. guile	g. uncalled-for
8. gullible	h. not planned
9. hackneyed	i. sly trickery
10. haphazard	j. easily fooled
	k. secret

FILL IN THE BLANK

Use the new words in the following sentences.

1. With a _____ move, the sophomore slipped the test answers to his roommate.

2. It took an editorial about security in the school's newspaper to _____ the campus into action.

3. "How could you be so _____ as to purchase an alleged Rolex watch from a street merchant?" her father asked.

4. In fables, foxes are noted for their _____.

5. Just like a squirrel, I plan to _____ my resources for the winter of my old age.

6. Knowing that he couldn't pass the exam, Tom rushed through the short answers in a _____ fashion.

7. I was planning for a quiet ride to the airport, but a _____ taxi driver had other plans.

8. _____ advice is rarely accepted.

9. By the time we had decoded the _____ telegram, it was too late to do anything about it.

10. Spencer's _____ plot put all of the film critics to sleep.

TRUE OR FALSE

Based upon the way the new words are used, identify the following sentences as T (True) or F (False).

1. Rover looked around furtively before burying the bone.

2. Adele's term paper was so garbled that it was a pleasure to read it.

3. Garrulous people can be boring because they rattle on and on.

4. Selecting numbers haphazardly, the sisters managed to be successful at the roulette table.

5. We complimented Lorenzo upon the hackneyed elements in his poems.

REVIEW EXERCISES: LESSONS 11-15

ANALOGIES

Each question below consists of a pair of related words or phrases, followed by five lettered pairs of words or phrases. Select the lettered pair that best expresses a relationship similar to that in the original pair.

1. DORMANT:AWAKE::
   - (A) stout:muscular   (B) stagnant:still
   - (C) egregious:flagrant   (D) ephemeral:evanescent
   - (E) wasteful:frugal

2. EULOGY:SPEECH::
   - (A) no-hitter:baseball game   (B) fledgling:professional
   - (C) survey:conclusion   (D) sincerity:tenderness
   - (E) effrontery:composure

3. DOGMATIC:BLAND::
   - (A) compatible:dissipated   (B) authoritarian:passive
   - (C) austere:caustic   (D) dilatory:tardy
   - (E) whimsical:capricious

4. ENIGMA:DETECTIVE::
   - (A) aberration:fisherman   (B) feast:despot
   - (C) dream:psychiatrist   (D) affinity:mathematician
   - (E) crystal ball:clairvoyant

5. EXPUNGE:ERASE::
   - (A) sprint:shuffle   (B) denounce:project
   - (C) rinse:cleanse   (D) defeat:conquer
   - (E) detonate:smother

6. EPHEMERAL:NEWSPAPER::
   - (A) informational:encyclopedia   (B) suspenseful:book
   - (C) entertaining:recording   (D) comforting:phone call
   - (E) tragic:play

7. GUILE:SWINDLER::
   - (A) chisel:carpenter   (B) regulation:contestant
   - (C) disparity:tailor   (D) disdain:receptionist
   - (E) catharsis:surgeon

8. ENHANCE:MAKE GREATER::
   (A) corroborate:inform (B) condone:reject
   (C) disperse:scatter (D) embroil:desecrate
   (E) ameliorate:augment

9. FORMIDABLE:FOE::
   (A) gullible:amendment (B) conciliatory:ambush
   (C) frugal:budget (D) altruistic:essay
   (E) circumspect:punishment

10 EBB:FLOOD::
   (A) erupt:forest (B) faint:shock
   (C) cajole:harmony (D) subside:anger
   (E) coalesce:demeanor

ANTONYMS

Choose the word or phrase that is most nearly *opposite* in meaning to the word in capital letters.

1. HACKNEYED: (A) wise (B) original (C) trifling
   (D) transported (E) abstract

2. GARBLED: (A) dramatic (B) institutional (C) feeble
   (D) clear (E) potent

3. FALLACY: (A) truth (B) value (C) boredom
   (D) inspiration (E) abuse

4. FORTUITOUS: (A) erratic (B) vile (C) discouraging
   (D) unfortunate (E) planned

5. EXACERBATE: (A) criticize (B) improve
   (C) praise highly (D) overrule (E) apologize

6. EXTOL: (A) belittle (B) wail (C) uplift
   (D) rupture (E) heal

7. FACILITATE: (A) hinder (B) replace (C) advocate
   (D) exchange (E) adapt

8. ENERVATE: (A) strengthen (B) reject (C) tarnish
   (D) modify (E) dilute

9. ELUCIDATE: (A) trounce (B) give in (C) confuse
   (D) call a halt (E) extend

10. DUPLICITY: (A) loss of confidence (B) elegance
    (C) act of clemency (D) modification
    (E) honesty

HEADLINES

Select the words which fit best in the newspaper headlines below.

1. VOLCANO THOUGHT TO BE _____ ERUPTS
   (ECLECTIC, ESOTERIC, DORMANT, FITFUL)

2. MEDALS AWARDED FOR _____ SERVICE TO THE NAVY
   (EXEMPLARY, ESOTERIC, EXPEDIENT, EVANESCENT)

3. WITNESS TENDS TO _____, LAWYER PROTESTS
   (EFFACE, ELUCIDATE, EQUIVOCATE, GALVANIZE)

4. MICROPHONES PICK UP EMBARRASSING _____RE-MARK
   (HAPHAZARD, GARRULOUS, GRATUITOUS, FORMIDABLE)

5. BOXER TO FACE MOST _____ CHALLENGE
   (EXPEDIENT, FURTIVE, FORMIDABLE, EGREGIOUS)

6. COURTEOUS BUREAUCRAT TREATS EVERYONE WITH _____
   (DUPLICITY, FRUGALITY, EQUANIMITY, GUILE)

7. CANDIDATES SEEK TO _____ENDORSEMENTS FROM FORMER STATE OFFICIALS
   (FACILITATE, EXTOL, EMBELLISH, GARNER)

8. _____ OVERSIGHT THREATENS BUDGET STABIL-ITY
   (EGREGIOUS, DORMANT, FORTUITOUS, EXPEDIENT)

9. DROUGHT CONDITIONS IN MIDWEST NOT RELIEVED BY _____ RAINS
   (FATUOUS, FLAGRANT, ESOTERIC, FITFUL)

10. COLLEGE PRESIDENT CRITICIZED FOR _____ POSI-TION
    (DOGMATIC, ECLECTIC, EFFERVESCENT, EXEMPLARY)

LESSON 16

■ hedonist ■ heretic ■ hierarchy ■ homogeneous ■ hyperbole
■ hypocritical ■ hypothetical ■ iconoclast ■ immaterial ■ imminent

hedonist *n.* one who lives solely for pleasure.

An avowed *hedonist*, Livingston is quick to extol the virtues of retirement in Tahiti.

"I'm interested in life and liberty, of course," said the *hedonist*, "but I'm dedicated to the pursuit of happiness."

Abandoning her lifestyle as a *hedonist*, Maria entered a convent.

heretic *n.* a person who upholds religious doctrines contrary to the established beliefs of his church. (By extension, heretic may be used to describe a person who holds an unpopular belief.)

Severely chastised for being a *heretic*, Brother Vincent was asked to leave the monastery.

Despite the lack of tangible evidence, he was accused by the Inquisition of being a *heretic*.

The editorial labeled the writer as a *heretic* for his criticism of our foreign policy.

hierarchy *n.* organization by rank, class, or grade.

In the company's *hierarchy*, I'm low man on the totem pole.

By means of guile, Drew reached the top of the *hierarchy* in his union.

In reorganizing church leadership, the elders developed a new and formidable *hierarchy*.

homogeneous *adj.* similar; uniform in nature.

The Shore Road School finds that *homogeneous* grouping of pupils facilitates learning.

My Army Reserve unit was a *homogeneous* one, since we all came from the same Ohio suburb.

Community activists were galvanized when they learned about the furtive plan to integrate the *homogeneous* housing project.

hyperbole *n.* an exaggerated statement used as a figure of speech for rhetorical effect.

Ione uses *hyperbole* when galvanizing her sales force into a frenzy of selling.

Knowing that "Garrulous Gary" was fond of *hyperbole*, we discounted most of what he had to say.

The tributes at Adrian's retirement dinner were filled with flagrant examples of *hyperbole*.

hypocritical *adj.* insincere; pretending to be what one is not.

I found it *hypocritical* of the judge to be involved in an illegal activity.

The minister was labeled *hypocritical* by his former assistant, who claimed the minister affected more religious devotion than he actually possessed.

Some have accused newspaper publishers of being *hypocritical* when they accept cigarette advertising while speaking against tobacco use in editorials.

hypothetical *adj.* supposed; assumed.

Saying that he has an aversion to *hypothetical* questions, the governor refused to reply.

I concocted a *hypothetical* situation as an expedient to resolving the issue.

During the conference, we engaged in playing roles, arbitrating conflicts, and coping with *hypothetical* problems.

iconoclast *n.* a person who attacks cherished beliefs or established institutions.

The philosopher didn't mind being called a heretic and an *iconoclast* because he was firm in his beliefs.

When she shook up the conservative law firm, Gloria earned the reputation of being an *iconoclast*.

Calling himself an *iconoclast*, the head of the school board questioned the value of the traditional reading lists.

immaterial *adj.* insignificant; unimportant.

Any activity which didn't involve gourmet food or luxurious living was regarded as *immaterial* by the hedonist.

The prosecutor objected to the attorney's exhibit, disparaging it as amateurish and *immaterial*.

Even my gullible uncle recognized Ida's argument as inconsequential and *immaterial*.

imminent *adj.* about to occur.

When Vatican reporters spied the smoke, they knew that the selection of a new Pope was *imminent*.

In the hypothetical problem presented to us, a nuclear war was *imminent*.

The ominous clouds told us that a storm was *imminent*.

SPOTLIGHT ON

heretic This word, meaning one who has adopted religious doctrines contrary to the established beliefs of his church, can be traced back to a Greek word which meant "taking" or "choosing." In short, the selection of such a far-out position is embodied in a disparaging sense in *heretic*.

iconoclast A picture image of Christ, or an angel or saint, usually painted on wood or ivory is known as an "icon," and is venerated in the Eastern Church. One who smashes such an object is an *iconoclast*, from the Greek word which meant "breaking an image." In modern times, you may be called an iconoclast if you attack a cherished belief which you think is foolish or wrong. We can see the similarity between iconoclasts and heretics.

MATCHING

Match the words in Column A with their definitions in Column B.

A	B
1. hedonist	a. similar
2. heretic	b. assumed
3. hierarchy	c. attacker of beliefs; image-breaker
4. homogeneous	d. pleasure-seeker
5. hyperbole	e. exaggeration
6. hypocritical	f. organization by rank, class or grade
7. hypothetical	g. about to happen
8. iconoclast	h. one who rejects church doctrine
9. immaterial	i. tolerant
10. imminent	j. unimportant
	k. insincere

FILL IN THE BLANK

Use the new words in the following sentences.

1. In a _____ speech, the executive told his staff to follow his actions while ignoring his public statements.

2. The playboy's reputation of being a _____ was well-deserved.

3. Although quite religious as a teenager, Mary Margaret developed into a _____ in her later years.

4. The youngster's previous criminal record was declared _____ by the judge.

5. Realizing that the ringing of the bell was _____, we started to close our notebooks and our minds.

6. Irene showed that she was an _____ by pointing out that the emperor had no clothes.

7. The reading group was _____ because all of the youngsters were two years below grade level.

8. To say that Mickey Mantle was the greatest baseball player of all time is to resort to _____.

9. For the purposes of illustration, Professor Nagler presented us with a _____ situation.

10. Detective Lynch wasn't privy to decisions being made by the _____ in her division.

TRUE OR FALSE

Based upon the way the new words are used, identify the following sentences as T (True) or F (False).

1. Accused of being a heretic, the editor vigorously defended his criticism of church doctrine.

2. The imminent surgeon was called upon to do the delicate brain operation.

3. Marlowe was an iconoclast, and no company tradition was safe from his attack.

4. Lawyer Karnes set up a hypothetical situation in which the witness was induced to incriminate himself.

5. When a speaker revels in hyperbole, I'm usually suspicious of his claims.

LESSON 17

immutable *adj.* never changing.

My father's *immutable* optimism can be traced back to the pleasant atmosphere in my grandmother's home.

Princess Charlotte is an *immutable* hedonist, forever yachting and partying with the rich and the famous.

Recognizing that Cabot was an *immutable* heretic, we didn't try to convert him.

impartial *adj.* fair; just; showing no favoritism.

An *impartial* attorney was asked to serve as a judge in the dispute.

The decision was apparently an *impartial* one, and we couldn't quarrel with it.

A baseball umpire has to be completely *impartial.*

impassive *adj.* without feeling or emotion; insensible.

Good poker players are supposed to maintain *impassive* appearances.

It was hard to remain *impassive* as we listened to the speaker's flagrant hyperbole.

Spartans were admired for their *impassive* demeanor even in the face of pain.

imperturbable *adj.* not easily excited or disturbed.

We couldn't believe that Rafael would be that *imperturbable* in the midst of a riot.

People frequently compliment Orientals for being *imperturbable.*

When the *imperturbable* student realized that his graduation was imminent, he finally showed some emotion.

implausible *adj.* not having the appearance of truth or reason.

The hypothetical case which Dan presented was so *implausible* that we refused to deal with it.

Only the most gullible member of our club would accept the *implausible* alibi.

It's *implausible* that with a homogeneous group we should get such heterogeneous results.

inadvertent *adj.* not done on purpose; careless.

I regarded the *inadvertent* comment as immaterial, but it proved to be significant.

An *inadvertent* technical error almost impaired the entire status of the space program.

Harlan demanded that the *inadvertent* slip be expunged from the official transcript.

incipient *adj.* in an early stage.

Dr. Hollinger, who is quite articulate, was able to describe the *incipient* ulcer in great detail.

The rookie's flagrant error spelled doom for his *incipient* career.

Economic realities forced the *incipient* enterprise to capitulate and close its doors.

incisive *adj.* keen; penetrating.

Incisive criticism by the newspaper's film reviewer led us to a renewed appreciation of the movie.

Following Huntley's *incisive* analysis, the bond traders were immediately galvanized into a frenzy of selling.

Cheryl's *incisive* coverage of City Hall affairs made her a formidable candidate for a Pulitzer Prize.

incongruous *adj.* inappropriate; out of place.

Seeing the little boy in a room filled with basketball giants struck me as totally *incongruous*.

We make an *incongruous* couple because I'm talkative and my wife is shy.

The Rembrandt painting seemed *incongruous* on a wall filled with modern art.

incontrovertible *adj.* not able to be disputed or denied.

It's *incontrovertible* that a settlement of the bitter strike is imminent.

Ryan offered *incontrovertible* evidence to show that his former partner was embroiled in a crass extortion scheme.

The Los Angeles Lakers offer *incontrovertible* proof that team play in basketball is a criterion for success.

SPOTLIGHT ON

incisive When you incise, you cut or carve. To make an incision is to cut or penetrate. An incisor is a cutting tooth. All of those words are related to *incisive*, from the Latin verb *cadere* or "to cut."

incongruous The Latin word *congruentem* means "coming together, agreeing." In geometry, we talk of congruent triangles which coincide exactly. When something is *incongruous*, therefore, it lacks harmony, is out of place, inappropriate.

MATCHING

Match the words in Column A with their definitions in Column B.

A	B
1. immutable	a. unmoved
2. impartial	b. calm
3. impassive	c. not showing favoritism
4. imperturbable	d. careless; negligent
5. implausible	e. far-fetched
6. inadvertent	f. unquestionable
7. incipient	g. out of place
8. incisive	h. acute
9. incongruous	i. unchangeable
10. incontrovertible	j. diligent
	k. just beginning

FILL IN THE BLANK

Use the new words in the following sentences.

1. Showing an actual bull on Wall Street is an _____ vision of an advertising agency.

2. It's _____ that patients are uneasy in August when psychiatrists traditionally take their vacations.

3. Before the _____ corporation could show a profit, the bank foreclosed on their mortgage.

4. Throughout the heated controversy, Albert remained _____ and aloof.

5. Despite all of our arguments, Maxine remained _____.

6. Felix's _____ report was lauded by management for its conciseness and wisdom.

7. I never fail to make at least one _____ mistake when I try to balance my checking account.

8. State auditors thought it _____ that the exact attendance percentages would be repeated for six months.

9. Throughout the crisis, Morgan remained _____ and encouraged the rest of us not to panic.

10. Nurse Campbell was seemingly _____, but she was actually quite sensitive to the suffering she saw.

TRUE OR FALSE

Based upon the way the new words are used, identify the following sentences as T (True) or F (False).

1. Vincent is so immutable on the topic of smoking that it's easy to influence him.

2. My broker amazed me by remaining imperturbable throughout the long day of the market crash in 1987.

3. It was difficult for the beauty contestant's family to remain impartial during the contest.

4. If the incipient plague could be nipped in the bud, health officials would be ecstatic.

5. Allan's weather prediction was so incisive that we guessed he had been trained as a meteorologist.

LESSON 18

■ incorrigible ■ indefatigable ■ indigent ■ ingratiate ■ innocuous
■ inscrutable ■ insipid ■ insurgent ■ intemperate ■ intractable

incorrigible *adj.* too firmly fixed to be reformed or changed.

Harry's *incorrigible* habit of smoking has impaired our relationship.

An *incorrigible* liar, Jill's face is impassive even when she's telling a giant whopper.

Our city has set up a special school for *incorrigible* youngsters who prevent others from learning.

indefatigable *adj.* tireless.

Edith's *indefatigable* efforts as a volunteer at the nursing home were extolled by the Sisterhood's president.

Known as an *indefatigable* defender of civil rights, the congressman garnered unanimous support for his bill.

The Narcotics Squad was *indefatigable* in infiltrating the seemingly impregnable drug syndicate.

indigent *adj.* poverty-stricken. (When used as a noun, *indigent* means someone who is poor or impoverished.)

Every Thanksgiving, the despot publicized his gift of turkeys to *indigent* families.

Once a wealthy and formidable boxer, Rocco is now *indigent* and quite forlorn.

The survey looked for a correlation between *indigent* students and poor achievers.

ingratiate *v.* to make oneself acceptable.

I tried to *ingratiate* myself with Maurice but he was immutably set against my proposal.

It's useless to attempt to *ingratiate* yourself with the foreman because he prefers to keep aloof from those on the assembly line.

The bouquet of roses was Joe's scheme to *ingratiate* himself with Marilyn, and it worked!

innocuous *adj.* harmless.

Who would have thought that my *innocuous* little remark would have embroiled us in a feud?

The not so *innocuous* whisper, a gratuitous insult, failed to ruffle our imperturbable host.

According to George, it's incontrovertible that one *innocuous* whiskey before dinner can't hurt you.

inscrutable *adj.* so mysterious that it cannot be understood.

We looked to Dora for a positive reaction, but her face was *inscrutable*.

The *inscrutable* note was no help to us in solving the enigma.

The meaning of "Rosebud" was *inscrutable* until the audience saw it on Citizen Kane's boyhood sled.

insipid *adj.* lacking interest or spirit.

In a devastatingly incisive review, one critic disparaged the novel as *insipid* and boring.

Wally's *insipid* personality was the antithesis of his charismatic sister's.

The cocktail party guests were engaged in *insipid* conversation.

insurgent *n.* one who rises in revolt. (Also used as an adjective; e.g., insurgent forces.)

Government representatives questioned the *insurgent* sharply but he remained silent and impassive.

During his late teens, Doug saw himself as an *insurgent* against the power structure.

With clandestine help from his friends, the *insurgent* made his escape from the prison.

intemperate *adj.* lacking in self-control.

Intemperate at the dinner table, Hudson's weight ballooned to 300 pounds.

Would you be considered *intemperate* if you drank too many cocktails?

We found Elliot's outburst *intemperate* and treated him with disdain for the rest of the evening.

intractable *adj.* hard to manage; not easily treated.

The *intractable* colt ran off rather than be saddled.

Because the girls were so adamant, immutable, and *intractable*, we finally acceded to their wishes.

Dr. Clemente was puzzled by the *intractable* infection.

SPOTLIGHT ON

insipid This is not a flattering adjective since it means "dull and colorless" when applied to a person or thing. The actual Latin meaning, however, is "not tasty." When we say that someone is "dull as dishwater," we're indicating that he's *insipid*—certainly not tasty.

intractable People who are obstinate, stubborn, adamant, and inflexible are said to be *intractable*. The origin, as with so many of our words, is Latin where the meaning is "cannot be handled." Whereas you may be called intractable for not bowing to someone else's wishes, in your mind you are usually "firm" or "committed." It all depends on what side of the argument you are on.

MATCHING

Match the words in Column A with their definitions in Column B.

A	B
1. incorrigible	a. poor; needy
2. indefatigable	b. bring oneself into favor
3. indigent	c. worthy of being redeemed
4. ingratiate	d. dull; colorless
5. innocuous	e. a rebel
6. inscrutable	f. incomprehensible
7. insipid	g. stubborn
8. insurgent	h. never getting tired or giving up
9. intemperate	i. excessive
10. intractable	j. beyond being reformed
	k. harmless

FILL IN THE BLANK

Use the new words in the following sentences.

1. Declaring Ricky _____, the school's principal vowed to suspend him indefinitely.

2. Seeing the bureau chief's _____ expression, I didn't know whether I'd be fired or promoted.

3. Mother Teresa received many awards for her _____ opposition to misery, poverty, and hunger.

4. As soon as my _____ remark was made, I could have kicked myself for being tactless.

5. Dominick's landlord is _____ about not renewing his lease.

6. The big ninth inning rally started quietly with an apparently _____ base hit.

7. Once she was recognized as an _____, Carmen joined the other young rebels in her division.

8. The only way you can _____ yourself with Mr. Romano is to do well on his tests.

9. Scholarship awards for youngsters from _____ families were funded by a number of altruistic organizations.

10. We were lulled to sleep by the _____ documentary dealing with Roumanian agriculture.

TRUE OR FALSE

Based upon the way the new words are used, identify the following sentences as T (True) or F (False).

1. For his indefatigable work on the campaign trail, Lewis was extolled by the candidate.

2. The stage play was so insipid that we were on the edge of our seats with excitement.

3. A humble apology was offered by the editor for the intemperate column published last week.

4. Indigent people are treated sympathetically by a benevolent Dutch government.

5. Dorcas took an intractable position against mercy killing, and we couldn't change her mind.

LESSON 19

■ irrefutable ■ irrelevant ■ jargon ■ judicious ■ kindle ■ labyrinth
■ lackluster ■ laconic ■ lampoon ■ lassitude

irrefutable *adj.* cannot be disproved.

The prosecutor shook the defense with the *irrefutable* argument that three people witnessed the murder and could identify the killer.

Technological advances have forced us to question theories that were once thought to be *irrefutable*.

People of faith see *irrefutable* proof of the hand of God in human destiny.

irrelevant *adj.* not to the point; not relating to the subject.

The judge instructed the jury to ignore the *irrelevant* testimony.

Betty's opinion of the dress is *irrelevant*, considering her obvious poor taste.

Her writing suffers from an emphasis on *irrelevant* details.

jargon *n.* the specialized vocabulary of members of a group.

The club members adopted a *jargon* that made them feel exclusive.

The *jargon* of sports writers is bright, sharp, and exciting.

Martin likes to use the *jargon* of the ignorant street hood, but in reality he is a clever and capable conversationalist.

judicious *adj.* wise; careful; showing sound judgment, prudent.

Gary thought it more *judicious* to speak to his mother rather than his father about extending his curfew time.

A *judicious* approach to the use of drugs would weigh the long-term risks against the fleeting pleasure of the moment.

A *judicious* investment he made when the children were toddlers now provided for their college tuition.

kindle *v.* to ignite; to arouse or inspire; to catch fire; to become aroused.

With the wind blowing so furiously, Ted found it difficult to *kindle* a fire.

Mr. Danby managed to *kindle* student interest in independent reading by providing class time, a variety of books, and awards as incentives.

Whenever Mrs. Gladstone heard another story about her grandson, a warm glow would *kindle* her gentle face.

labyrinth *n.* a maze; a complicated, perplexing arrangement or course of affairs.

Once inside the cave, the searchers were confronted with a *labyrinth* that defied them to find the route to the wounded explorer.

Greg decided against majoring in philosophy, finding it a *labyrinth* which would only confuse him.

After leading the class through a *labyrinth* of hypotheses, Professor Lander emerged with a crystal-clear explanation.

lackluster *adj.* lacking brightness; dull; lacking liveliness, vitality or enthusiasm.

His *lackluster* response to our suggestions made us lose our initial enthusiasm.

After a *lackluster* road trip, the team caught fire when they returned to the home field.

The *lackluster* applause indicated to the comedian that he was no Bob Hope.

laconic *adj.* brief or terse in speech; using few words.

The tense situation called for a *laconic* reply, not a lengthy exposition.

Harriet's *laconic* speech gave her a reputation for wisdom.

If Maria were as frugal with her money as she is *laconic* with her words, she would be a rich woman today.

lampoon *n.* strong, satirical writing, usually attacking or ridiculing someone.

The college quarterly featured a *lampoon* of fraternity hazing.

Tim found it easy to *lampoon* his classmates but hard to find a friend.

To *lampoon* teachers has become the favorite pastime of the failing student.

lassitude *n.* state or feeling of being tired and listless; weariness.

Because of the depression over his injury, Ronald lapsed into a state of *lassitude*.

Lassitude comes from a feeling of hopelessness.

The long flight and the jet lag brought on a *lassitude* of several days duration.

SPOTLIGHT ON

jargon One meaning of *jargon* is akin to "slang," which usually starts out as sub-standard usage but may in time be upgraded to acceptability. *Jargon* is also related to *dialect*, which is the language that is peculiar to a particular region or group and does not have a derogatory connotation.

labyrinth In Greek mythology, Daedalus built an intricate network of winding passages within a cave to house the Minotaur, a creature that was half-man and half-bull. King Minos of Crete had to feed seven youths and seven maidens annually to this monster until Theseus finally slew him and escaped from the *labyrinth* with the help of Ariadne, the king's daughter.

MATCHING

Match the words in Column A with their meaning in Column B.

A	B
1. irrefutable	a. spiritless
2. irrelevant	b. satire
3. jargon	c. prudent
4. judicious	d. official
5. kindle	e. unquestionable
6. labyrinth	f. intricacy
7. lackluster	g. specialized vocabulary
8. laconic	h. concise
9. lampoon	i. inapplicable
10. lassitude	j. sluggishness
	k. light

FILL IN THE BLANK

Use the new words in the following sentences.

1. A simple no is the most _____ negative response I can give.

2. Though the _____ aimed some vicious barbs at him, Fred tried to retain his sense of dignity.

3. He _____ their hopes of victory with his rousing speech.

4. As the pendulum swung back and forth, a general _____ overcame those who had volunteered to be hypnotized.

5. We were duly impressed with Miranda's _____ logic.

6. Computerese, pedagogese and pidgin English are examples of _____.

7. The brain is a _____ with unfathomable secrets.

8. You can discount most of Lynn's remarks as _____.

9. The coach's halftime pep talk jolted the team out of its _____ attitude.

10. A _____ compromise may be preferable to a hollow victory.

TRUE OR FALSE

Based on the way the new words are used, identify the sentences as T (True) or F (False).

1. Calvin's frequent use of electronics jargon made his meaning unmistakably clear to the audience.

2. The candidate's former position as a union official was entirely irrelevant to his electability in the blue collar district.

3. Henry's lackluster performance in the preliminaries eliminated him from the competition.

4. The lampoon of the university president in the student newspaper was a grievous error.

5. Overcome by a feeling of lassitude, Brent charged through the defense and scored a touchdown.

LESSON 20

latent *adj.* present but invisible or inactive; lying hidden and undeveloped.

AIDS researchers have discovered there is a *latent* period for the disease during which time tests would not give an indication of the presence of the virus.

Marilyn's *latent* charm came to the fore after she got a few tactful pointers from her sister.

The appearance of the famous actor at the school awakened Lisa's *latent* interest in a stage career.

laudable *adj.* worthy of praise. (The related verb *laud* means "to praise.")

Despite the pressure of coping with a hostile crowd, Mark made a *laudable* showing in his relief effort on the mound.

Admitting his error in misjudging the new employee was a *laudable* act on Mr. Brinkley's part.

The board rewarded Ellen's *laudable* achievements by promoting her to chief executive officer.

lethargic *adj.* drowsy; dull; sluggish; indifferent.

Eating a heavy meal tends to make me *lethargic*, which may explain why I become a couch potato after a big dinner.

The strain of working long hours on a labyrinth of problems had a *lethargic* effect on the young scientist.

The debilitating illness left Paul in a *lethargic* state.

levity *adj.* lightness; lack of seriousness; fickleness.

Brad's *levity* contrasted sharply with his roommate's solemnity.

There's nothing like a little judicious *levity* to ease the strain after tense negotiations.

Such *levity* is improper on this serious occasion.

listless *adj.* indifferent; marked by a lack of energy or enthusiasm.

We had expected him to be full of enthusiasm and were surprised by his *listless* attitude.

Mark's friends tried to rouse him from his *listless* frame of mind.

The counselor attributed Penny's *listless* and lackluster performance in school to the illness of her mother.

lucid *adj.* easily understood; rational; clear; clear-minded.

After a few moments of unintelligible ravings, Mr. Turner became *lucid* again.

The lecturer's *lucid* explanation left no question unanswered.

Laconic speech is not necessarily less *lucid* than lengthy discourse.

malicious *adj.* spiteful; intentionally mischievous or harmful. (The noun form *malice* means "active ill will" or "spite.")

The *malicious* behavior of the accused brought a stern reprimand from the judge, who then imposed the maximum penalty.

The widespread and pointless destruction in the house left no doubt as to the *malicious* intent of the burglar.

The *malicious* con man led the widow through a labyrinth of schemes to deprive her of her fortune.

marred *adj.* injured; spoiled; damaged; disfigured.

The fight in the corridor *marred* Lorna's otherwise perfect record as a model student.

The beauty of the graceful statue was *marred* by the incongruous graffiti scrawled over it.

Marlo thought her freckles *marred* her appearance, but her family assured her they were among her best features.

meager *adj.* thin; lean; of poor quality or small amount.

The visiting team lampooned the *meager* dinner served by their hosts.

The survivors of the shipwreck clung to the desperate hope that their *meager* rations would last till they were rescued.

Israel, with its *meager* resources, has tapped the skills and intelligence of its people to build a viable economy.

meandering *adj.* winding back and forth; rambling.

We spent a pleasant afternoon sailing on the *meandering* stream.

Dr. Feller had a habit of *meandering* from one subject to another until his conversation became totally irrelevant.

Meandering through the crowded streets of a foreign city is my idea of a tourist's delight.

SPOTLIGHT ON

latent Though at first glance *latent* may appear to be related to *late*, the two words do not have a common origin. The former is derived from a Latin root meaning "hidden," while the latter comes from an Old English word meaning "slow" or "tardy."

lethargic In Greek mythology, Lethe was the river of forgetfulness. Drinking its waters produced loss of memory and a condition of apathy and laziness that we associate with lethargy.

MATCHING

Match the words in Column A with their definition in Column B.

A	B
1. latent	a. sluggish
2. laudable	b. scanty
3. lethargic	c. potential
4. levity	d. twisting
5. listless	e. evil
6. lucid	f. clear-minded
7. malicious	g. passive
8. marred	h. commendable
9. meager	i. botched
10. meandering	j. flavorful
	k. lack of seriousness

FILL IN THE BLANK

Use the new words in the following sentences.

1. Coffee is supposedly a stimulant, but it tends to make me more _____.

2. What is most _____ about Raymond's performance is his total immersion in his role.

3. One could not accuse little Dennis of _____ conduct, but that was small comfort to Mr. Pellegrino, who was out some $500 for the vase Dennis broke.

4. The picture made the intricate subject more _____ than pages of description.

5. It was not until she was in her senior year that Esmeralda's _____ intellectual abilities came to the fore.

6. We spent a quiet afternoon _____ through the labyrinth of streets in the quaint town.

7. An altercation over the seating arrangement _____ the opening ceremonies at the graduation.

8. Dr. Urquart was not given to _____, but she was known to smile a lot.

9. The least harsh criticism I can offer is that Raymond gave, at best, a _____ performance.

10. Harold had to work evenings to supplement his _____ stipend.

TRUE OR FALSE

Based upon the way the new words are used, identify the following sentences as T (True) or F (False).

1. The lethargic athlete bounded up the four flights of stairs without stopping for breath.

2. Lucy had the annoying habit of meandering from one subject to another without rhyme or reason.

3. What marred the performance was the exquisite beauty of the soprano.

4. Mr. Danforth polished off the last morsel of his six course meal and gratefully announced, "This was the most malicious meal I've had in weeks."

5. Jed's meager savings were hardly enough to start him off in business.

REVIEW EXERCISES: LESSONS 16-20

ANALOGIES

Each question below consists of a pair of related words or phrases, followed by five lettered pairs of words or phrases. Select the lettered pair that best expresses a relationship similar to that expressed in the original pair.

1. IMMATERIAL:SUBSTANTIAL::
   - (A) lustrous:gleaming   (B) dominant:influential
   - (C) loyal:treacherous   (D) cordial:warm
   - (E) capricious:devious

2. HYPERBOLE:TRUTH::
   - (A) fable:story   (B) exaggeration:understatement
   - (C) patriarch:commoner   (D) fanatic:orthodox
   - (E) beneficiary:heir

3. IMPASSIVE:NONCHALANT::
   - (A) imperative:pressing   (B) jumbled:blended
   - (C) elastic:durable   (D) literal:bookish
   - (E) maternal:related

4. INCIPIENT:CLIMACTIC::
   - (A) innovative:modified   (B) stubborn:vacillating
   - (C) fearful:ashamed   (D) pinkish:blood-red
   - (E) liberal:educated

5. INDIGENT:PRIVATION::
   - (A) admiral:defeat   (B) invalid:weakness
   - (C) merchant:bankruptcy   (D) athlete:sprain
   - (E) voter:ballot

6. INNOCUOUS:TOXIC::
   - (A) dangerous:contaminated   (B) early:tardy
   - (C) homely:hideous   (D) shapely:slovenly
   - (E) gloomy:rude

7. LEVITY:PARTY::
   - (A) passivity:prison   (B) officiousness:workplace
   - (C) decorousness:house of worship
   - (D) vanity:athletic field   (E) argument:conference

8. IRRELEVANCE:EXTRANEOUS::
   (A) transaction:profitable (B) omen:fortuitous
   (C) vanity:flirtatious (D) retreat:heraldic
   (E) din:cacophonous
9. LABYRINTH:PERPLEXING::
   (A) circus:tantalizing (B) sky:infinite
   (C) theatre:dramatic (D) religious service:uplifting
   (E) garden:tiring

10. LAUDABLE:VILE::
    (A) discontented:quarrelsome (B) admirable:prepared
    (C) eventful:memorable (D) committed:engaged
    (E) charming:disagreeable

ANTONYMS

Choose the word or phrase that is most nearly *opposite* in meaning to the word in capital letters.

1. HERETIC: (A) benefactor (B) pagan (C) skeptic
                   (D) conformist (E) saint

2. HYPOTHETICAL: (A) transitional (B) puzzling (C) actual
                   (D) productive (E) mythical

3. IMMUTABLE: (A) mutual (B) loquacious
                   (C) complaining (D) disreputable
                   (E) variable

4. INGRATIATE: (A) inhibit (B) alienate (C) appease
                   (D) oppose (E) persevere

5. INSCRUTABLE: (A) cunning (B) dull (C) obvious
                   (D) admirable (E) indifferent

6. INTEMPERATE: (A) sober (B) persuasive (C) irritable
                   (D) gallant (E) keen

7. IRREFUTABLE: (A) unsure (B) open to question
                   (C) changeable (D) unnatural
                   (E) beguiling

8. LACONIC: (A) responsive (B) wordy (C) spherical
                   (D) plain (E) idiomatic

9. LATENT: (A) apparent (B) conscientious
                   (C) insightful (D) periodic (E) hasty

10. LUCID: (A) free (B) humorous (C) bitter
                   (D) scatter-brained (E) reluctant

HEADLINES

Select the word that fits best in the newspaper headlines below.

1. _____ COMPROMISE ENDS LEGAL IMPASSE
   (LACKLUSTER, LACONIC, JUDICIOUS, IMMINENT)

2. _____ OF GOVERNOR BRINGS OFFICIAL REPRIMAND
   (JARGON, LAMPOON, HYPERBOLE, MEANDERING)

3. _____ BUILDS PLEASURE PALACE
   (LABYRINTH, HEDONIST, JARGON, LASSITUDE)

4. INCUMBENT EXPECTS _____ DEFEAT
   (IMMINENT, IMPASSIVE, IRRELEVANT, IRREFUTABLE)

5. MAYOR REMAINS _____ AMID RIOTS
   (IMPERTURBABLE, IRREFUTABLE, IMPLAUSIBLE, MALICIOUS)

6. CRITICS PAN PLAY AS TOO _____
   (INCISIVE, LUCID, INSIPID, LATENT)

7. HOLIDAY CELEBRATION _____ BY HEAVY DOWNPOUR
   (MEANDERING, LAMPOONED, INGRATIATED, MARRED)

8. SPEECH EXPERT PUBLISHES PAPER ON _____ IN THE WORKPLACE
   (JARGON, HEDONIST, HYPERBOLE, LABYRINTH)

9. MURDERED MAN LEAVES _____ MESSAGE
   (INTRACTABLE, INSCRUTABLE, LISTLESS, INCIPIENT)

10. FAMILY WITH HEART ADOPTS YOUNGSTER LABELED
    _____

    (INCISIVE, INCONTROVERTIBLE, INCORRIGIBLE, LETHARGIC)

LESSON 21

■ meticulous ■ mitigate ■ morose ■ nomenclature ■ nonchalance
■ obliterate ■ obscure ■ obsolete ■ officious ■ opportunist

meticulous *adj.* very careful about details; fussy.

Sidney was *meticulous* about his clothing but quite sloppy about his room.

A *meticulous* investigation into the tragic hazing incident resulted in a suspension of the fraternity.

Even though Thomas was generally laconic in his speech, he was *meticulous* about explaining in great detail his part in the heroic rescue of his friend.

mitigate *v.* to make or to become milder or less severe; to moderate.

The doctor assured Mrs. Shiller that the medicine would *mitigate* her pain in a short time.

After a lackluster defense, the attorney noted her client's youth in an attempt to *mitigate* the expected harsh sentence.

The principal told the student delegation that to *mitigate* the punishment for bringing weapons into the school would only invite serious trouble.

morose *adj.* gloomy; bad-tempered.

When we come across someone who is both loquacious and *morose*, we are in for a double portion of unpleasantness.

What marred Ralph's chances to develop friendships was not only his *morose* attitude but his impatience with every innocent display of levity.

Joan's *morose* nature makes her always expect the worst.

nomenclature *n.* a systematic naming in an art or science.

The *nomenclature* can be quickly mastered by using memory devices

The first step in tackling a new topic is to learn its *nomenclature*, which is a kind of shorthand of its key concepts.

The emergence of new theories in psychology will undoubtedly lead to a revision of the *nomenclature* in the field.

nonchalance *n.* carelessness; lack of interest or concern.

Edward's *nonchalance* about his studies made it difficult to lampoon him about his poor showing in the midterm exams.

The family had grown to love the adopted child and could not accept with *nonchalance* the order to return her to her natural mother.

Nonchalance is not part of Angela's fiery temperament.

obliterate *v.* to blot out leaving no traces; to destroy.

The authorities feared that the heavy rain would *obliterate* all signs of the escaped prisoner.

One ill-spoken word can *obliterate* a carefully built up friendship.

The bombardment failed to *obliterate* the stubborn resistance of the encircled company.

obscure *adj.* not clear or distinct; hidden; remote; not well known. (When used as a verb, *obscure* means "to make dark, dim, or indistinct," or "to conceal or hide as if by covering.")

Far from the well-traveled highway was an *obscure* village that seemed to belong to another age.

The teacher had the gift of making his students see the beauty in even the most *obscure* poetry.

In his clever but unprincipled way, the devious attorney managed to *obscure* the issue with irrelevant facts.

obsolete *adj.* out-of-date.

Propeller planes have become *obsolete*.

Dr. Clemens' frequent use of *obsolete* words and expressions typed her as archaic, to say the least.

Dr. Samuel Johnson once remaked that he had retained clothing which had become *obsolete* and later returned to fashion.

officious *adj.* meddling; giving unnecessary or unwanted advice or services.

Mr. Klar's *officious* manner helped him gain friends easily but lose them in short order.

Those who tend to be *officious* do not know the value of independent action.

An *officious* person is likely to be bumbling and ineffective.

opportunist *n.* one who takes advantage of any opportunity without regard for moral principles.

The Bible captures the essence of the *opportunist* in the description: "Every man doing what is right in his own eyes."

The *opportunist* is so anxious to get ahead that he is ready to ignore the needs, feelings and welfare of his fellow man.

Sharon did not realize that Harold's interest in her was that of an *opportunist* who saw her as a means of improving his position in her father's company.

SPOTLIGHT ON

nonchalance This word comes to us via French from the Latin *calere*, meaning "to be warm." It is easy to see the relationship to *calorie*, the heat needed to raise the temperature of one gram of water one degree Centigrade—and, in less scientific terms, the source of all the extra baggage we sometimes carry around.

obsolete The difference between *obsolete* and *obsolescent* is that the latter refers to something that is on its way out while the former has attained that unenviable status. Often, the line between the two is a matter of opinion.

MATCHING

Match the words in Column A with their definitions in Column B.

A	B
1. meticulous	a. casualness
2. mitigate	b. passé (out of fashion)
3. morose	c. dim
4. nomenclature	d. finicky
5. nonchalance	e. reliable
6. obliterate	f. depressed
7. obscure	g. unscrupulous person
8. obsolete	h. relieve
9. officious	i. erase
10. opportunist	j. naming
	k. nosy

FILL IN THE BLANK

Use the new words in the following sentences.

1. The _____ of computer science has given us a new version of an old joke: Computer scientists never die; they go a byte at a time.

2. Try as he did, Michael could not _____ the memory of the tragic accident.

3. When the family finally met Miriam, they understood why David was so _____ about dressing for his date with her.

4. Our _____ outlook quickly changed when our team took the lead with two touchdowns in the opening minutes of the second quarter.

5. The proof that Mr. Bartok was a(n) _____ was irrefutable when we learned he had framed his partner in order to gain sole ownership of the property.

6. We often associate being _____ with a bureaucratic busy-ness that seeks to take the longest possible route to go from point A to point B.

7. Understanding the cause of misbehavior may serve to _____ our criticism and help us to find ways of preventing it.

8. Miguel's contrived _____ about his breakup with Rosita didn't fool us one bit.

9. A(n) _____ reference in the letter to a stranger the victim met on a ship was the clue the detective was looking for.

10. Only a dead language avoids the problem of dealing with _____ words.

TRUE OR FALSE

Based on the way the new words are used, identify the following sentences as T (True) or F (False).

1. By following directions with meticulous care, Sol was able to complete the experiment without any difficulty.

2. Monoplanes have become obsolete but may still be seen in museums.

3. Officious people are generally well-liked because they are so helpful.

4. Lawson was an opportunist who worshipped only the mighty dollar.

5. A man of morose temper can be counted on to be the life of the party.

LESSON 22

■ opulent ■ overt ■ painstaking ■ pariah ■ parsimonious
■ partisan ■ paucity ■ peerless ■ perceptive ■ perfidy

---

opulent *adj.* wealthy; abundant.

The *opulent* family chose to spend money for the public benefit rather than for private indulgences.

The hungry man was speechless when he saw the *opulent* banquet table set before the King.

Mr. Garner admitted to being *opulent*, but he claimed credit for his foresight in choosing the right family to be born into.

overt *adj.* not hidden; open.

Most observers took the senator's speech as an *overt* bid for his renomination.

Nothing could obscure the fact that Nicholas had been apprehended in an *overt* act of stealing.

Without any *overt* statement, the couple made it plain that they intended to get married despite the parents' disapproval.

painstaking *adj.* very careful; diligent.

Researchers are engaged in a *painstaking* effort to find a vaccine against the AIDS virus.

Thomas Edison's remark about genius being composed of one percent inspiration and 99 percent perspiration suggests that *painstaking* work is more crucial than luck.

Lt. Muñoz directed the *painstaking* search for the missing child.

pariah *n.* an outcast.

The Western mind finds it difficult to accept the idea of a *pariah* class.

Anyone who breaks the code of honor at West Point is treated like a *pariah*.

In the past, ignorance and fear conspired to place the label of *pariah* on lepers, who were forced to live in special colonies separated from contact with mainstream society.

parsimonious *adj.* too thrifty; stingy.

Government should not be *parsimonious* with its college grant program, for students will repay the investment with tenfold benefit to the country.

Dickens' Scrooge, before his metamorphosis, is regarded as the prototype of the *parsimonious* man.

No matter how *parsimonious* Mr. Fleming was, it did not mitigate his fear that he would die a poor man.

partisan *adj.* showing a strong support for a party or cause; characteristic of a guerrilla fighter.

A national crisis demands ignoring *partisan* politics and opportunism.

The speaker, following the *partisan* line, meticulously avoided comment on the proposed tax increase.

Juanita approached each challenge with a *partisan* fervor.

paucity *n.* scarcity; smallness in number or amount.

The *paucity* of rain in the Midwest will cause a serious food shortage in the months to come.

Mr. Micawber, eternally optimistic, regarded his *paucity* of funds as merely a temporary inconvenience.

Gulliver realized that the Lilliputians' *paucity* of intellect matched their size.

peerless *adj.* having no equal; better than the rest.

Theresa's *peerless* beauty was admired by all who saw her.

If you can overlook Albert's officious manner, you will find him an otherwise *peerless* character.

The great actress was awarded the "Tony" for her *peerless* performance.

perceptive *adj.* discerning; observant; sensitive.

Having a *perceptive* nature, Jason was able to sense the child's embarrassment even before she uttered a sound.

Father was *perceptive* to our needs and keyed his advice to our strengths and weaknesses.

Shakespeare is often praised for being so *perceptive* to the nuances of language.

perfidy *n.* treachery; betrayal of trust.

The double agent was obviously a man capable of acts of *perfidy*.

Literature has no better example of *perfidy* than the conduct of King Lear's elder daughters.

A person in whose soul *perfidy* lurks cannot be at peace.

SPOTLIGHT ON

opulent The Latin root of this word, *op-*, is the operative part of such words as *opus*, and *operate*. Does this perhaps suggest the best way to become opulent?

pariah *Pariah* is the Tamil word for a drum. The pariah, a member of one of the lowest castes in India, was a hereditary drumbeater. It is almost as if the poor pariah was fated to warn off others from approaching him.

MATCHING

Match the words in Column A with their definitions in Column B.

A	B
1. opulent	a. shortage
2. overt	b. public
3. painstaking	c. miserly
4. pariah	d. mystery
5. parsimonious	e. affluent
6. partisan	f. deceit
7. paucity	g. hard-working
8. peerless	h. astute
9. perceptive	i. outsider
10. perfidy	j. adherent
	k. incomparable

FILL IN THE BLANK

Use the new words in the following sentences.

1. Why, asked the two-headed man from Mars, are they treating me here like a(n) _____.

2. Operating deep in enemy territory, the _____ group made its presence felt through countless acts of sabotage.

3. _____ of material possessions is not as much a curse as our discontent with what we have.

4. The lecturer was _____ enough to adapt his speech to the interests of his teenage audience.

5. My idea of a(n) _____ vacation is having a wide circle of friends and the time and opportunity to enjoy their company.

6. _____, like poverty, is a crucible to test our mettle.

7. _____ is the constant fear of one who has tried to buy friendship and loyalty.

8. We must base our opinions on _____ actions rather than on winks, nods or tacit understandings.

9. Edmund Burke differentiated between the _____ and the economical person, praising the latter not for saving but for being selective.

10. _____ detective work paid off when a parking ticket led to the capture of the killer known as Son of Sam.

TRUE OR FALSE

Based upon the way the new words are used, identify the following sentences as T (True) or F (False).

1. The pariah was greeted with shouts of joy by the entire population of the town.

2. The court could not ignore Lester's overt admission of guilt.

3. Benedict Arnold's perfidy endeared him to all his countrymen.

4. In an attempt to lower the price, the wily merchant scoffed at the peerless gem, saying it was probably not worth more than the paper it was wrapped in.

5. Penury or opulence—it matters little to those dedicated to a spiritual life.

LESSON 23

- peripheral ▪ peruse ▪ philistine ▪ piety ▪ pique ▪ placate
- placid ▪ plagiarize ▪ platitude ▪ pompous

peripheral *adj.* external; incidental; tangential.

Stick to the facts and don't waste time on *peripheral* issues.

Mr. Clayton realized that the banker was concentrating on *peripheral* matters and painstakingly avoiding the subject of the loan.

A *peripheral* remark can sometimes mask a primary intention.

peruse *v.* to study; to read.

Margaret tried to *peruse* the letter when she thought she was not being observed.

The students were directed to *peruse* the poem not just for its language but for its ideas.

Jim could not *peruse* the rejection notice without a shudder.

philistine *adj.* narrow-minded; smugly conventional. (When used as a noun, *philistine* means "a dull often priggish person guided by material rather than intellectual or artistic values.")

Philistine stubborness should not prevent us from advancing ourselves intellectually.

Walter, comfortable in his *philistine* straitjacket, closed his mind to any innovative suggestion.

George's refusal to listen to any music except rock 'n roll typed him as a *philistine*.

piety *n.* devotion and reverence, especially to God and family. (Closely related to this noun is the adjective *pious*, meaning "devout, zealous in performing religious obligations." It also has the uncomplimentary meaning of "seemingly virtuous or affecting virtue hypocritically.")

Mrs. Billings is noted for her *piety* and philanthropy.

The parson set an example of *piety* and humility that was admired by the entire community.

It is not the outward show of *piety* that counts but the faith that lies in the heart.

pique *v.* to hurt the feelings of or make resentful; to arouse or excite. (When used as a noun, *pique* means "a temporary feeling of wounded vanity; a fit of resentment.")

Raising taxes to help balance the budget will only *pique* the national temper.

To *pique* her students' curiosity, Ms. Garson told them she had a surprise in store for them before the day was over.

Anna's show of indifference was intended to *pique* the interest of her new suitor.

placate *v.* to soothe; to pacify.

It is no mean feat to *placate* an enemy without yielding ground.

After voting for the unpopular bill, the congressman had to *placate* public opinion.

The offer of a trip to the circus helped to *placate* the screaming child.

placid *adj.* outwardly calm or composed; self-satisfied; peaceful.

The medication made the hyperactive child not only *placid* but almost catatonic.

Though the partisan was outwardly *placid* when he saw the cruel treatment of the refugees, inwardly he was seething with rage.

Mrs. Wiggins' *placid* acceptance of her penury freed her from the malicious consequence of jealousy.

plagiarize *v.* to take ideas or writings from someone else and present them as one's own; to use without giving credit.

Jordan knew better than to *plagiarize* a peerless sonnet of Shakespeare, but he foolishly hoped his teacher would not recognize it.

The professor warned Marion not to *plagiarize* the report when he saw the paucity of footnotes in her term paper.

Ben insisted he did not *plagiarize* the song though he admitted there were some similarities between the popular "Summer Evening" and his "Evening Song."

platitude *n.* a thought or remark that is dull, trite, flat or weak.

Muriel's speech was so full of *platitudes* that you felt you were listening to a record.

Professor Thomson, committed as he was to an opulent vocabulary, would never stoop to utter a *platitude*.

Many a *platitude* still contains the wisdom of the common folk.

pompous *adj.* self-important; stately; magnificent; excessively ornate.

The *pompous* doorman refused to admit the disheveled woman.

The overbearing politician alienated the common people with his *pompous* speeches.

The loquacious taxi driver could not elicit a smile from the *pompous* passenger.

SPOTLIGHT ON

peruse   Originally the word had the connotation of examining in detail or scrutinizing. Hence, one meaning was "to read carefully and thoroughly." However, in a gradual shift that began to look upon the word as pretentious, *peruse* now often suggests a casual or leisurely reading. Your choice.

placate   There are a number of interesting idioms that describe a situation connected with the act of placating an enemy and turning him into a friend. These range from "meeting someone halfway," "holding out the olive branch," and "kissing and making up," to "smoking the peace pipe," "burying the hatchet," and "pouring oil on troubled waters." Keep these in mind when it's time to placate an irate person.

MATCHING

Match the words in Column A with their definitions in Column B.

A	B
1. peripheral	a. devoutness
2. peruse	b. unruffled
3. philistine	c. harmony
4. piety	d. relatively unimportant
5. pique	e. cliché
6. placate	f. provoke
7. placid	g. boorish
8. plagiarize	h. appease
9. platitude	i. arrogant
10. pompous	j. pore over
	k. usurp

FILL IN THE BLANK

Use the new words in the following sentences.

1. Melissa apologized for the accusations she made in a moment of _____.

2. It took a good measure of tact to _____ Phil for making him feel like a pariah.

3. Lucy's _____ smugness might just be an expression of her fear of failure in attempting anything new.

4. The expression on her father's face as he began to _____ her report card told her he was proud of her achievement.

5. The court had a difficult time determining whether the single bar of music in both compositions was an overt attempt to _____ or a simple coincidence.

6. The librarian had a _____ sneer that obliterated any inclination to talk above a whisper.

7. The chairman interpreted the flurry of _____ questions as an overt attempt to filibuster.

8. The preacher never guessed that he was losing his audience because of his _____-filled sermons.

9. The paucity of generous contributions did not ruffle the _____ optimism of Reverend Stokes.

10. The evangelist's outward show of _____ could not forever hide his hypocrisy.

TRUE OR FALSE

Based on the way the new words are used, identify the following sentences as T (True) or F (False).

1. Mr. Markow's philistine upbringing propelled him into the sophisticated world of the literati.

2. In a fit of pique at her husband, Grace blurted out that she wished she had remained single.

3. The babysitter tried to placate the child by promising her that she could stay up until her parents returned.

4. The placid waters raged on, overflowing the river bank.

5. Hubert was awarded the prize for submitting "the best plagiarized essay" in the class.

LESSON 24

ponderous *adj.* very heavy; bulky; labored and dull or tiresome.

Modern science has not yet solved the mystery of how the Aztecs were able to lift *ponderous* stones with their meager tools.

The *ponderous* furniture did not fit in at all with the elegance and light decor of the room.

The knight's *ponderous* suit of armor restricted his movement.

pragmatic *adj.* practical; opinionated; concerned with actual practice rather than with theory or speculation.

The public opinion poll has been accepted as a *pragmatic* way of determining the thinking of the people at a given point in time.

The *pragmatic* solution to the problems of integration lies not in the study of peripheral issues but in taking concrete steps that lead to the desired results.

For all his professed piety, Mr. Carlson, judged by *pragmatic* standards, did nothing to help the poor by uttering pompous platitudes.

preclude *v.* to make impossible; to shut out; to prevent.

Luis perused the plan many times to *preclude* the chance that he had missed something.

Colin was piqued that a previous commitment would *preclude* her accepting the invitation.

To *preclude* the possibility of being charged with plagiarism, Denise made sure to cite her sources fully.

precocious *adj.* having or showing much more ability or knowledge than is usual at such a young age; early or prematurely ripe or developed.

The father was extremely proud of his *precocious* child when he saw her excellent report card.

The *precocious* Mozart is said to have composed music at the age of three.

107

Not all *precocious* youngsters achieve the success predicted for them in later life.

prestigious *adj.* honored; having an illustrious name or reputation.

With the backing of the *prestigious* Friar's Club, it was easy to raise the money for the new hospital wing.

The family carried the *prestigious* name of one of the Mayflower settlers.

The *prestigious* Ivy League colleges naturally have higher admission standards.

pretentious *adj.* claiming or demanding a position of distinction or merit; showy; self-important.

The teacher immediately recognized the *pretentious* style as a flagrant attempt to hide a plagiarism.

Geraldine suspected the young man as a *pretentious* fraud, but that did not preclude her from falling for his charm and polish.

The *pretentious* young author spoke as if he had already been enshrined in the hall of fame.

procrastinate *v.* to put off doing something until a later time; to delay.

Joe was so lazy that his teachers constantly warned him not to *procrastinate*.

If we fail to make an immediate decision and continue to *procrastinate*, the problem will snowball until it becomes unmanageable.

The question is, did Hamlet *procrastinate* in revenging his father's murder because of a weakness of character or a lack of conviction?

prodigious *adj.* enormous; extraordinary; marvelous.

There was a *prodigious* outpouring of sympathy from the entire community for the bereaved family.

The critics hailed the revival of the Greek play as a *prodigious* success.

Umberto's parents became alarmed at the *prodigious* amount of food he consumed, but the doctor assured them it was just a normal, healthly adolescent appetite.

profane *adj.* secular; not holy; not connected with religion; irreverent.

Please refrain from using *profane* language in this holy place.

At one time there was hardly any *profane* art, as most artists worked under the aegis of the church.

The pious benefactor withdrew his support of the show because of its *profane* treatment of the Biblical story.

profusion *n.* abundance; a great or generous amount; extravagance.

Marigolds and violets grew in *profusion* along the sides of the road.

Luckily we did not believe Mr. Brander's story which was laced with a *profusion* of lies.

Henrietta was so popular because she was blessed with a *profusion* of wit and charm.

SPOTLIGHT ON

pragmatic Alexander the Great is perhaps the supreme example of the pragmatist. Confronted with the Gordian knot, which an oracle had revealed would be undone by the future master of Asia, Alexander simply cut it with his sword to claim his destiny.

prestigious The etymology of this word brings us to "juggler's tricks" and "illusions," a far cry from its modern positive connotation of honor and glory. Some words have all the luck!

MATCHING

Match the words in Column A with their definitions in Column B.

A	B
1. ponderous	a. temporal
2. pragmatic	b. defer
3. preclude	c. unwieldy
4. precocious	d. furious
5. prestigious	e. influential
6. pretentious	f. plenty
7. procrastinate	g. boastful
8. prodigious	h. utilitarian
9. profane	i. ripening before its time
10. profusion	j. immense
	k. restrict

FILL IN THE BLANK

Use the new words in the following sentences.

1. The philistine may be loath to admit that ideas spun out by theoretical physicists may prove to be of _____ value.

2. Mr. Clinton was eulogized as one who achieved the proper balance between the _____ and the holy elements of his life.

3. A _____ wave crashed across the bow and engulfed the fragile vessel.

4. Stella was trying to decide between a post with the diplomatic corps and a less _____ job teaching in a small midwestern college.

5. Remember that a failure in your first attempt should not _____ your trying again.

6. This child is too _____ to placate with a lollipop.

7. The predicted landslide victory turned out to be a _____ illusion.

8. The _____ stories meandering through thousands of pages have given way to the tightly-knit narrative that can be read in a few hours.

9. Deidre began her letter of apology with these words: "I could not _____ any longer."

10. Claude tried to buy popularity by providing a _____ of parties.

TRUE OR FALSE

Based upon the way the new words are used, identify the following sentences as T (True) or F (False).

1. The only way to get a job done is to procrastinate.

2. The loss of this game will preclude us from reaching the finals.

3. The benefit brought a huge crowd because prestigious names appeared on the program.

4. Bert was not concerned because he was certain his prodigious error would be forgiven.

5. After all his pretentious claims, Professor Hall was exposed as a graduate of a mail order diploma mill.

LESSON 25

■ prolific ■ propensity ■ provincial ■ prudent ■ pugnacious
■ quandary ■ querulous ■ quixotic ■ raconteur ■ rancor

prolific *adj.* producing many offspring; producing much; abundant.

Rabbits are notoriously *prolific*.

Irving Berlin is a *prolific* songwriter.

In recent years, Japan and the Soviet Union have been more *prolific* in the sciences than the United States.

propensity *n.* a natural leaning or tendency; bent.

Miguel has a *propensity* for making friends easily.

The twins' *propensity* to excel in music must be an inherited trait.

Steve hoped his puppy would soon outgrow her *propensity* for getting into mischief.

provincial *adj.* having the ways and speech of a certain province; of or like country people as apart from city people (unsophisticated); thinking in narrow ways.

The *provincial* capital of the country was the site of the prodigious fair.

The *provincial* quality of the candidate's speech precluded his acceptance by the average voter.

On their first visit to the capital in thirty years, the *provincial* couple thought they had entered a new world.

prudent *adj.* careful or cautious in a sensible way; wise; frugal.

As a child Clara was not precocious academically but quite *prudent* in her choice of friends.

Prudent laws make for a safe society.

With *prudent* management Nicholas turned his meager savings into a small fortune.

pugnacious *adj.* eager and ready to fight; quarrelsome.

For the benefit of those who are *pugnacious*, let us repeat what Benjamin Franklin said: There never was a good war or a bad peace.

We profane our souls when we adopt a *pugnacious* attitude toward our fellow humans.

Robin was pragmatic enough to restrain his *pugnacious* instinct when faced by a stronger rival.

quandary *n.* condition of being doubtful or confused.

The benefits and dangers of a nuclear plant leave us in a *quandary*.

Being in a *quandary* may be more unsettling than facing a painful truth.

Carol said she would relish being in the *quandary* of having accepted two dates for the same evening.

querulous *adj.* peevish; faultfinding; expressing or suggestive of complaint.

We tend to turn a deaf ear to *querulous* demands for attention.

Bob adopted a *querulous* tone that certainly did not ingratiate him with his host.

Ironically, the more toys the child was given, the more *querulous* he became.

quixotic *adj.* idealistic and utterly impractical.

It is *quixotic* to think that we can ignore the environmental consequences of pollution.

Mr. Romley spun a rather *quixotic* scenario for his future that was based on his winning the lottery.

The scientist insisted his scheme was neither *quixotic* nor pretentious but pragmatic and within reach.

raconteur *n.* a person skilled at telling stories or anecdotes.

Comedians and masters of cermonies must be consummate *raconteurs*.

Mark Twain was an accomplished *raconteur*, able to hold his audiences spellbound for hours.

The *raconteur* decided to end his story because of the lateness of the hour.

rancor *n.* deep spite or malice; strong hate or bitter feeling.

The president said he harbored no *rancor* against Congress for overriding his veto.

A forgiving heart will save you from the corrosive effects of *rancor*.

Lincoln appealed to his countrymen to put *rancor* and vengeance behind them and heal the nation's wounds.

SPOTLIGHT ON

prolific Related to *proletarian*, *prolific* refers to the lowest social and economic class of a community. This brings to mind the famous Lincoln remark that God must have loved the common people since he made so many of them.

quixotic The main character in Miguel de Cervantes' 17th century novel, Don Quixote de la Mancha is a well-meaning but deluded hero who goes through a series of misadventures. He is best remembered as the deranged knight who tilts at (charges against) windmills, thinking they are giants. The word *quixotic* is based on this character.

MATCHING

Match the words in Column A with their definitions in Column B.

A	B
1. prolific	a. perplexity
2. propensity	b. fruitful
3. provincial	c. constructive
4. prudent	d. insular
5. pugnacious	e. impractical
6. quandary	f. spinner of yarns
7. querulous	g. whining
8. quixotic	h. resentment
9. raconteur	i. partiality
10. rancor	j. combative
	k. discreet

FILL IN THE BLANK

Use the new words in the following sentences.

1. It is unfair to attribute Mr. Sorrell's _____ remarks to his advanced age.

2. When she was alone, Mrs. Danley indulged in _____ flights of fancy, imagining herself young and beautiful again, with the world at her feet.

3. Whether he was speaking to children in grade school or to inmates in prison, the _____ knew just how to pitch his story.

4. Clyde's propensity for both basketball and baseball left him in a _____ as to what sport to choose for his career.

5. Even in the most prestigious company, Sir Timothy could not shed his _____ manners.

6. The gorilla may look _____ but it is usually a peaceful, herbivorous creature.

7. The partnership broke up with a _____ that left deep scars on their psyches.

8. The _____ footnotes made the book ponderous reading.

9. Faced with an embarrassing situation, Debra took the _____ course and apologized for her officious remark.

10. Victor's _____ to procrastinate brought him to the verge of failure.

TRUE OR FALSE

Based upon the way the new words are used, identify the following sentences as T (True) or F (False).

1. Mr. Farrel, a prudent man, refused to sign the contract until he had read the small print.

2. His extraordinary output of a book a year tells you that James Michener is one of the most prolific writers of our time.

3. The rancor that existed between the couple guaranteed that there would be a happy ending to their squabble.

4. Phil's pugnacious demeanor may be a cover-up for his inferiority complex.

5. Gladys' skill as a raconteur was readily apparent as she captured our attention with her first words.

REVIEW EXERCISES: LESSONS 21-25

ANALOGIES

Each question below consists of a pair of related words or phrases, followed by five lettered pairs of words or phrases. Select the lettered pair that best expresses a relationship similar to that expressed in the original pair.

1. NOMENCLATURE:NICKNAME::
   - (A) arena:space (B) castle:hovel
   - (C) heart:ticker (D) music:jazz
   - (E) howitzer:artillery

2. OPPORTUNIST:UNSCRUPULOUS::
   - (A) clown:morose (B) humorist:entertaining
   - (C) bigot:unfriendly (D) hunter:nimble
   - (E) hypocrite:demonstrative

3. PARSIMONIOUS:MONEYGRUBBER::
   - (A) clumsy:bungler (B) dictatorial:manager
   - (C) mischievous:child (D) patronizing:bookworm
   - (E) wealthy:golfer

4. PEERLESS:INCOMPARABLE::
   - (A) provocative:philosophical (B) whimsical:funny
   - (C) impulsive:primitive (D) subjective:fair
   - (E) inquisitive:curious

5. PERIPHERAL:CARDINAL::
   - (A) loquacious:laconic (B) immense:sufficient
   - (C) comforting:relaxing (D) alienated:intense
   - (E) flimsy:flaky

6. PHILISTINE:MATERIALISTIC::
   - (A) hostage:merciful (B) swimmer:muscular
   - (C) daredevil:adventurous (D) sprinter:slow
   - (E) composer:melodic

7. PRAGMATIC:SERVICEABLE::
   - (A) voluntary:appointed (B) muscular:competitive
   - (C) regal:inherited (D) charitable:philanthropic
   - (E) married:engaged

8.   PRODIGIOUS:GOLIATH::
     (A) aged:grandfather   (B) tiny:Tom Thumb
     (C) mountainous:Everest   (D) mathematical:Euclid
     (E) spiral:tube
9.   PROLIFIC:STERILE::
     (A) deceitful:hidden   (B) scholarly:forgetful
     (C) foolish:tricky   (D) taxing:refundable
     (E) medicinal:poisonous

10. PRUDENT:RASH::
     (A) melodious:peppy   (B) metallic:shiny
     (C) trace:artistic   (D) indifferent:heedful
     (E) stationary:literal

ANTONYMS

Choose the word or phrase that is most nearly *opposite* in meaning to the word in capital letters.

1. OBLITERATE: (A) educate   (B) overlook   (C) promise
                   (D) restore   (E) obligate

2. OBSCURE: (A) well done   (B) haphazard   (C) critical
                   (D) absurd   (E) famous

3. PAINSTAKING: (A) cursory   (B) forceful   (C) bustling
                   (D) rewarding   (E) comforting

4. PERCEPTIVE: (A) exclusive   (B) vigorous   (C) shallow
                   (D) trustworthy   (E) ordinary

5. PIETY: (A) malice   (B) hunger   (C) irreverence
                   (D) purity   (E) lewdness

6. POMPOUS: (A) ill-bred   (B) repulsive   (C) cryptic
                   (D) distinctive   (E) sheepish

7. PRECOCIOUS: (A) punctual   (B) habitual   (C) frail
                   (D) late-blooming   (E) mature

8. PROFUSION: (A) summary   (B) scarcity
                   (C) unemployment   (D) ignorance
                   (E) brevity

9. PROPENSITY: (A) necessity   (B) aversion   (C) motivation
                   (D) antithesis   (E) pressure

10. QUIXOTIC: (A) contrary   (B) immature   (C) indecisive
                   (D) down-to-earth   (E) domineering

HEADLINES

Select the word that fits best in the newspaper headlines below.

1. _____ PLANE MAKES CROSS COUNTRY FLIGHT
    (PROVINCIAL, OVERT, OBSOLETE, QUERULOUS)

2. PRESIDENT ATTRIBUTES LOW POPULARITY RATING TO _____ DEBT
    (PAINSTAKING, PARSIMONIOUS, METICULOUS, PONDER-OUS)

3. INCUMBENT WINS ON STRENGTH OF _____ VOTING RECORD
    (PEERLESS, POMPOUS, OFFICIOUS, PROLIFIC)

4. BOSS CHIDES ASSISTANT FOR _____ HER PRIVATE MAIL
    (PROFANING, PERUSING, MITIGATING, PLAGIARIZING)

5. JUDGE DISALLOWS _____ TEMPERAMENT AS GROUNDS FOR DIVORCE
    (PRUDENT, PROFANE, MOROSE, PLACID)

6. FORMER CHILD STAR DISCOURAGED BY _____ OF ROLES
    (PLATITUDE, NONCHALANCE, PROFUSION, PAUCITY)

7. REBEL CENTRAL AMERICAN LEADER ACCUSED OF _____
    (PROPENSITY, PIETY, PERFIDY, QUANDARY)

8. DENUNCIATION BY PRIME MINISTER _____ COMPROMISE SOLUTION
    (OBSCURES, OBLITERATES, PROFANES, PRECLUDES)

9. _____ WAGER EARNS STUDENT FREE TUITION
    (PRETENTIOUS, PRUDENT, PARSIMONIOUS, POMPOUS)

10. MATRIMONIAL ADS _____ CURIOSITY OF 600 SUITORS
    (PLACATE, PERUSE, PIQUE, MITIGATE)

LESSON 26

■ raze ■ rebuff ■ recalcitrant ■ recluse ■ redundant ■ refurbish
■ rejuvenate ■ relegate ■ relic ■ remorse

raze *v.* to tear down completely; to destroy.

The corporation voted to *raze* the decaying structure and replace it with a modern skyscraper.

Unless we are prudent enough to start dredging operations immediately, erosion could *raze* our entire beachfront property.

The city was in a quandary whether to *raze* the convention hall with all its structural faults or pour more public funds into the necessary repairs.

rebuff *v.* to refuse in a sharp or rude way; to snub; to drive or beat back.

Because of its impracticality, we had to *rebuff* Elsie's suggestion, but we could have been gentler about it.

It was sheer luck that the outnumbered patrol was able to *rebuff* the enemy attack.

Seymour had a propensity to *rebuff* any invitation that did not advance his financial prospects.

recalcitrant *adj.* refusing to obey rules or follow orders; unmanageably resistant.

The mule is probably the most *recalcitrant* domesticated animal.

Tommy had a reputation for responding to orders with a pugnacious and *recalcitrant* rebuff.

The AIDS virus is one of the most *recalcitrant* problems medical science has had to confront.

recluse *n.* a person who lives alone, away from others.

Every neighborhood has its *recluse* about whom mysterious secrets are whispered.

Once his agoraphobia had been cured, the *recluse* turned out to be a person of great charm and a raconteur of marvelous tales.

Robinson Crusoe became a *recluse* not by choice but by the circumstance of a shipwreck.

redundant *adj.* wordy; exceeding what is necessary or normal; lavish; overflowing.

I wonder if authors who are called prolific are really merely *redundant*.

The judge called the witnesses's statement *redundant* and immaterial.

It is *redundant* to add "I think" after the phrase "in my opinion" for they mean the same thing.

refurbish *v.* to freshen or polish again; to make like new.

The agent promised to *refurbish* the apartment and put it in move-in condition within one month.

Mr. Stanton planned to *refurbish* the French provincial chair and to place it in his study.

"Why did you *refurbish* my house in my absence?" Florence asked querulously. "Didn't you realize it was filled with valuable antiques?"

rejuvenate *v.* to make young or fresh again.

The half-time pep talk helped to *rejuvenate* the team.

There was rancor in the sorcerer's heart when he saw that the potion could *rejuvenate* the king but left him old and decrepit.

The advertisement promised to *rejuvenate* your skin as you slept.

relegate *v.* to put in a less important position; to assign; to banish.

The slumping batter accepted without rancor his being *relegated* from clean-up position to eighth in the lineup.

Is it true that some masterpieces were actually *relegated* by the artists to their pupils?

The usual procedure is for the chairman to *relegate* the work to special committees.

relic *n.* a thing or part that remains from the past; something kept as sacred because it belonged to a saint.

Minna kept a closetful of *relics* from her family home in Kentucky.

The *relics* of ancient cities give us an idea of the culture of past civilizations.

Some consider a prison a *relic* of the medieval form of punishment that is retained because of the lack of an alternative.

remorse *n.* a deep feeling of sorrow or guilt over a wrong one has done.

Trudy felt *remorse* over having broken her promise.

The *remorse* we feel for hurting those we love somehow begins the process of reconciliation.

Roberta did not pretend to feel *remorse* for an action she considered justified.

SPOTLIGHT ON

relic Derived from the Latin word for "remains of a martyr," *relic* has over time acquired additional meanings. It now serves as a synonym for *souvenir* or *memento*. It also means "a vestige, a trace of some past or outmoded practice or custom."

remorse If you've ever felt like kicking yourself for something you've said or done that you shouldn't have, you know the literal meaning of *remorse*, which is derived from the Latin *re plus mordere*, "to bite again." For that matter, *smart*, meaning "painful hurt," has the same root. This suggests that actions that cause us *remorse* are not very smart.

MATCHING

Match the words in Column A with their definitions in Column B.

A	B
1. raze	a. renovate
2. rebuff	b. hermit
3. recalcitrant	c. demote
4. recluse	d. demolish
5. redundant	e. expand
6. refurbish	f. intractable
7. rejuvenate	g. self-reproach
8. relegate	h. spurn
9. relic	i. repetitious
10. remorse	j. keepsake
	k. reinvigorate

FILL IN THE BLANK

Use the new words in the following sentences.

1. Our dog must be a _____ by nature for he shuns the company of other dogs as if they belonged to another species.

2. Pompous speech tends to be _____.

3. Nothing can _____ like a dose of self-confidence.

4. _____ is a bitter pill to swallow but the healing wisdom it brings may last a lifetime.

5. There are societies which _____ the husband to a secondary role.

6. The legislators questioned the wisdom of the decision to _____ the historic courthouse.

7. When Gwen found she was stuck for an explanation about her absence, she planned to _____ her story about temporary amnesia that she had previously used with success.

8. A _____ can take the form of damning with faint praise.

9. Can you imagine the nerve of the hustler trying to sell me an Egyptian _____ with the "made in Japan" label clearly stamped on it?

10. The housing shortage has proved to be _____ to quick and easy solutions.

TRUE OR FALSE

Based on the way the new words are used, identify the following sentences as T (True) or F (False).

1. After the building was razed, it was completely refurbished.

2. The brief vacation helped Ms. Colter feel rejuvenated and ready to take on the world.

3. The relic, thought to have come from the Spanish galleon, fetched a handsome sum at the auction.

4. For his daring exploit, Commander Evans was relegated to the highest position in the navy.

5. The assemblyman welcomed the rebuff of his constituents and vowed to justify their faith in him.

LESSON 27

repudiate *v.* to reject; to refuse to recognize, acknowledge or pay; to divorce or discard.

The expert's testimony did not *repudiate* the collector's claim that the relic was authentic.

The contractor reluctantly agreed to refurbish the damaged portion of the building, but he indicated he would *repudiate* any further obligations.

Both sons sought to *repudiate* their father's will on the basis of the fact that he was a recluse who had lost touch with reality.

repugnant *adj.* disgusting; loathsome; objectionable; incompatible.

Bigotry is *repugnant* to the tradition of our nation.

The idea of slavery was so *repugnant* to the abolitionists that they felt no remorse about going to war to achieve their goal.

The delicacies of one culture may be *repugnant* to others.

rescind *v.* to cancel; to repeal; to set aside.

The people danced with joy when the government agreed to *rescind* the rule of apartheid.

The strikers rebuffed any calls to negotiate until management consented to *rescind* the firing of five employees.

The order to *rescind* the jail sentence resulted from the decision to relegate the offense to a misdemeanor.

residual *adj.* left over; remaining.

After the product had been distilled, there was a *residual* substance that baffled the chemist.

We learned too late that DDT and other insecticides have *residual* properties that cannot be easily counteracted.

The *residual* effect of the hazing generated a move to ban such initiations altogether.

resilient *adj.* getting back strength or spirits quickly; springing back into shape or position.

Blanca was so *resilient* that she was back on the field two weeks after the accident.

The NASA scientists are searching for a material that will be as *resilient* as rubber and yet as sturdy as steel.

With each blow he absorbed, the champ became less *resilient* until finally the referee stopped the fight.

respite *n.* a temporary cessation or postponement, usually of something disagreeable; interval of rest.

The union leader announced, "We are too close to victory to take a *respite* from our labors."

The condemned man was filled with rancor over the governor's refusal to grant him a *respite* from the severe sentence.

The candidate took a *respite* from his strenuous campaign to spend a few quiet days with his family.

reticent *adj.* not saying much, especially about one's thoughts.

Dominick was *reticent* about revealing his role in the robbery.

Though she had above average intelligence, Lisa was *reticent* about expressing her opinions in public.

"Come," Mr. Santos urged his *reticent* pupils, "there's no mistake like the fear of making mistakes."

retract *v.* to draw back or draw in; to take back a statement; to promise or to offer.

The drop in orders forced the company to *retract* the offer of an across-the-board raise for all the employees.

The counselor quickly learned that it is imprudent to *retract* a promise made to a five-year-old.

Dr. Gindi had to *retract* the skin around the wound in order to cleanse it.

ruthless *adj.* merciless; cruel; heartless.

Judge Randall imposed the maximum sentence on the *ruthless* killer.

The *ruthless* treatment of the adopted child aroused the conscience of the public, who clamored for laws to protect innocent victims.

Simon Legree stands out as the *ruthless* slavemaster in Harriet Beecher Stowe's classic novel, *Uncle Tom's Cabin.*

sagacious *adj.* very wise or shrewd. (The noun *sage* refers to one who is distinguished for wisdom, rich in experience, and sound in judgment.)

Glen turned to his father for advice, for he knew him to be *sagacious* and understanding.

The *sagacious* course is sometimes a matter of resorting to common sense, patience or humor.

When the count showed that Stella and Wendy tied for the presidency of the club, the members came up with a *sagacious* compromise—a presidium.

SPOTLIGHT ON

residual This word has proven very useful as a combining form in many fields, often to explain what cannot be otherwise fully accounted for. In chemistry, there is *residual* valence; in economics, residual claimant theory; in math, *residual* error; in physics, *residual* magnetism; and in government, *residual* power.

respite From the Latin *respectus,* "looking back," *respite* suggests that we ought to stop occasionally in the midst of our frenetic activity not only to recoup our strength but to examine where we have been and what we have done in order to plan our next move.

MATCHING

Match the words in Column A with their definitions in Column B.

A	B
1. repudiate	a. remnant
2. repugnant	b. draw back
3. rescind	c. pause
4. residual	d. buoyant
5. resilient	e. hateful
6. respite	f. insistent
7. reticent	g. abolish
8. retract	h. farsighted
9. ruthless	i. reserved
10. sagacious	j. to cast off publicly
	k. heartless

FILL IN THE BLANK

Use the new words in the following sentences.

1. The _____ benefits of Andrew's volunteer work went far beyond the immediate satisfaction of doing a good deed.

2. Dr. Mahoney said, "Mr. Kramer, remember that you have reached 70 and your body is not as _____ as it was at 40."

3. Not only did the dentist _____ the charge of malpractice, he vowed to countersue for defamation of character.

4. It is redundant to _____ a law that has been ignored for decades.

5. The revolutionaries wanted to raze the building that housed the _____ torture chambers.

6. Calvin understood that he would lose face if he tried to _____ the challenge he had made in the heat of anger.

7. Mrs. Long's decision to run for office transformed her from a _____ housewife to a garrulous firebrand.

8. The communist line rages against the _____ exploitation of the worker, but it is the laborer in the capitalist society who lives the better life.

9. When anger boils up in you and an explosion is imminent, the _____ thing to do is to step back and count to ten.

10. When the rescue workers heard faint voices coming from the rubble of the collapsed building, they worked without _____ until they freed the trapped children.

TRUE OR FALSE

Based on the way the new words are used, identify the following sentences as T (True) or F (False).

1. Meryl was pleased to find her blind date so repugnant.

2. The coach feared that the resilient team would be unable to overcome the embarrassing loss.

3. The gift was a ruthless act of charity that was deeply appreciated.

4. The pilot brought the plane to a safe stop despite the fact that the landing gear was stuck in a retracted position.

5. The governor rescinded her endorsement of the prison reform bill after learning that the cost would be double that of the estimate.

LESSON 28

salutary *adj.* healthful; useful or helpful; remedial.

Upon sagacious reflection, Simon realized that his parents' rebuke, though painful, was *salutary*.

We cannot repudiate the knowledge amassed by the ancients, for long before the advent of modern medicine, the *salutary* effects of certain herbs and minerals were already known.

Christine's early failure provided a *salutary* jolt to her assumption that study was unnecessary.

sanction *n.* authorized approval or permission; support or encouragement; something that gives binding force to a law. (As a verb, *sanction* means "to ratify or confirm; to authorize or permit.")

There is no *sanction* for murder in human society.

Without the *sanction* of the people's vote, the self-proclaimed leader was bound to fail in his massive reform program.

The law does not *sanction* the use of force or intimidation in the electoral process.

saturate *v.* to soak through and through; to fill completely.

What we need now, said the farmer, is a heavy rain that will *saturate* the soil for a good six inches.

The train wreck of the chemical tank cars *saturated* the area with toxic fumes, and the authorities called for a total evacuation until the residual effects were no longer dangerous.

The critic said the book was so *saturated* with innuendoes and distortions that the publisher would be well advised to rescind it.

savory *adj.* pleasing to the taste or smell; pleasant; morally attractive.

Mother could concoct a most *savory* dish out of the simplest ingredients.

I find no fruit more *savory* than luscious grapes.

126

Too late, Mr. Wallace discovered that his erstwhile partner was not a *savory* character.

scapegoat *n.* one taking the blame for the mistakes and crimes of others.

The proclivity to look for a *scapegoat* to absolve us of sin seems to be a universal trait.

Coach Fleming refused to look for a *scapegoat* to take the responsibility for the embarrassing defeat.

Billy maliciously made his brother the *scapegoat* for his setting fire to the garage.

scoff *v.* to mock or jeer at; to make fun of.

The fable of the fox and the grapes teaches that we tend to *scoff* at what we cannot attain.

It was Eugene's lack of exposure to the arts that led him to *scoff* at visits to the museums.

The clergyman said it happens, though rarely, that the person who comes to *scoff* remains to pray.

scrupulous *adj.* very honest and conscientious; careful about details; exact.

The IRS expects each taxpayer to keep a *scrupulous* record of claimed expenses.

Though Mr. Price was *scrupulous* in destroying every bit of evidence that could implicate him in the robbery, in the end he was betrayed by his jilted girlfriend.

No one suspected Sophia of the embezzlement, for she had a reputation for being *scrupulous.*

scrutinize *v.* to look at very carefully; to inspect minutely.

The umpire decided to *scrutinize* the ball after observing the strange movements of the pitcher.

The museum curator *scrutinized* the painting even more closely than usual, since there were some doubts about its authenticity.

The customs officials *scrutinize* the baggage of those passengers that experience and a sixth sense have taught them to suspect.

sectarian *adj.* pertaining to a group within a larger group that is limited by common beliefs or interests; narrow-minded.

New religious denominations developed as a result of *sectarian* differences within the church.

Lester's *sectarian* beliefs made it difficult for him to find acceptance in the small college he had chosen.

Louis has a *sectarian* perspective that is impervious to change.

sequester *v.* to hide or keep away from others; to withdraw into seclusion; to confiscate; to segregate.

With no verdict in sight, the judge issued the order to *sequester* the jury for the night.

The principal said, "Let's *sequester* the suspected troublemaker and see if the class functions any better."

The agent pointed out that the huge leafy trees will *sequester* the house and lend it an air of privacy and intimacy.

SPOTLIGHT ON

salutary *Salutary* is derived from the Latin *salus*, "health." The Roman satirist Juvenal recognized the connection between physical health and mental well being. Though we may hear of particularly courageous people whose mental powers seem to overcome physical disabilities, for most of us the maxim, "a sound mind in a sound body," holds true.

scapegoat The origin of this word is in the Hebrew *azazel*, meaning "the goat that departs." The Bible prescribes a service in which a goat upon whose head the sins of the people are symbolically placed is sent into the wilderness. The ceremony represented a public expression of atonement, just as the prayer and fasting on the Day of Atonement bespeaks the individual's desire to seek forgiveness.

MATCHING

Match the words in Column A with their definitions in Column B.

A	B
1. salutary	a. drench
2. sanction	b. examine thoroughly
3. saturate	c. conceal
4. savory	d. approval
5. scapegoat	e. principled
6. scoff	f. appetizing
7. scrupulous	g. clannish
8. scrutinize	h. beneficial
9. sectarian	i. oust
10. sequester	j. sacrifice
	k. ridicule

FILL IN THE BLANK

Use the new words in the following sentences.

1. On reviewing his speech, the congressman found it to be _____ and congenial and devoid of any statements that required a retraction.

2. Popular usage has been able to _____ expressions that language purists have railed against.

3. The raid uncovered a quantity of arms, drug paraphernalia and money, which the police had to _____ until the trial.

4. Immediate solutions must be found for the congested lanes and cars that _____ the space around our major airports.

5. Terrorists _____ at the laws of civilized society and consider everyone fair game to be sacrificed for their radical goals.

6. Demagogues usually find a _____ in a minority group which becomes the focal point of hatred and abuse and turns public attention away from the real source of the nation's troubles.

7. We generally do not _____ our own actions as often as we do those of others.

8. The artist copied the original with _____ care, then let the cat out of the bag by thoughtlessly signing his own name.

9. Jared was criticized for his _____ beliefs, but he remained faithful to the principles he had been taught to revere.

10. The latest medical advice holds that walking and swimming are more _____ exercises than jogging.

TRUE OR FALSE

Based on the way the new words are used, identify the sentences as T (True) or F (False).

1. The planes saturated the clouds with silver iodide in an effort to bring rain to the parched region.

2. There were many volunteers to be the scapegoat for it meant many honors with little risk.

3. The person who is too scrupulous about minor details may be avoiding coming to grips with the real problems.

4. The savory sauce was the secret ingredient of the delicious barbecued meat.

5. An honest lawyer will not scrutinize every line of a contract.

LESSON 29

■ serene ■ skeptical ■ sobriety ■ solemn ■ soporific ■ sporadic
■ spurious ■ squalid ■ stagnate ■ stoic

---

serene *adj.* unruffled; tranquil; unclouded.

The *serene* morning sky gave no hint of the downpour that would later saturate our cabana.

The owner of the fire-gutted boutique remained *serene* and dispassionate throughout the hair-raising ordeal.

The aged empress died with a *serene* expression on her gentle face.

skeptical *adj.* not easily persuaded or convinced; doubting the fundamental doctrines of religion.

Shirley cast a *skeptical* look at her father when she was told she had to be home by 11 o'clock.

We would be well advised to be *skeptical* if we are promised something for nothing.

Amanda's *skeptical* view of religion began to change as she delved more deeply into the Bible commentaries.

sobriety *n.* seriousness, gravity or solemnity; absence of alcoholic intoxication.

The extreme *sobriety* of five-year-old Veronica indicated a not very salutary sign of her social development.

Mr. Hynes, a scrupulous teetotaler, took special pride and delight in maintaining his *sobriety* while all around him an orgy of drinking was underway.

"If we look at the question of AIDS with all the *sobriety* it deserves," the mayor said, "we will stop looking for scapegoats and concentrate on finding a cure."

solemn *adj.* observed or done according to ritual or tradition; formal; serious or earnest; arousing feelings of awe; very impressive.

Before giving testimony in court, a witness is required to take a *solemn* oath that he or she will tell the whole truth.

Every November the American voters exercise their *solemn* right to choose their representatives.

Adopting a *solemn* tone, the college president exhorted the graduates to bring honor and pride to their alma mater.

soporific *adj.* causing sleep; drowsy.

Dr. Moran informed Mr. Amsel of the medicine's *soporific* effect and advised him not to drive for six hours after taking it.

Kenneth enjoyed the political science class, mostly because the *soporific* voice of the lecturer helped him catch up on his lost sleep.

As a result of the heavy meal and the *soporific* after-dinner speaker, a chorus of mild snoring pervaded the banquet hall.

sporadic *adj.* occurring at irregular intervals; isolated.

The distant *sporadic* gunfire kept the refugees awake throughout the night.

The Center for Disease Control allayed the public concern by announcing that the *sporadic* outbreak of the disease should not be interpreted as an epidemic.

The *sporadic* incidents of cheating at West Point bring dishonor to the institution.

spurious *adj.* lacking authenticity; counterfeit; false.

It was revealed that the correspondent who filed the *spurious* report had actually been sequestered at the time of the supposed interview.

The first lesson to keep in mind when dealing with *spurious* information is that all that glitters is not gold.

The administration hunted down a *spurious* copy of the chemistry final in an effort to determine its source.

squalid *adj.* dirty or wretched in appearance; morally repulsive; sordid.

The recluse lived in a *squalid* house on the edge of town and could not be persuaded to give it up for a more respectable domicile.

So many people live out their *squalid* lives in loneliness, poverty or sickness without the healing balm of a kind word from a sympathetic neighbor.

A wise man, seeing a home in *squalid* condition, remarked, "Dirt is not dirt, but only something in the wrong place."

stagnate *v.* to lie inactive; to fail to progress or develop.

The mind must not be allowed to *stagnate* for it is like a tool that becomes dull if it is not used.

"There is no middle road or standing still," the professor declared. "We either *stagnate* and retrogress, or we develop our talents and abilities and move forward."

Mr. Barrios' excuse for changing jobs every few years is that he does not wish to *stagnate* in one place.

stoic *adj.* indifferent to or unaffected by pleasure or pain; impassive.

Edward accepted the reprimand in *stoic* silence though he realized he was the scapegoat for the whole group.

A freshman at Yale who contended that he missed an exam because he "had a headache" was enlightened by this *stoic* advice: Most of the world's work is done by people who have headaches.

Job is perhaps the most outstanding example of *stoic* patience in the face of unimaginable adversity.

SPOTLIGHT ON

serene A less common definition of *serene* is "august or most high," as used in addressing a royal personage—Your Serene Highness. It suggests that one characteristic of majesty is the ability to remain calm and composed even under the most trying circumstances.

stoic The Greek Stoikas were members of a school of philosophy that held that all occurrences were the unavoidable result of divine will; hence, it was pointless to complain. Their attitude can be summed up as "Grin and bear it."

MATCHING

Match the words in Column A with their definitions in Column B.

A	B
1. serene	a. incredulous
2. skeptical	b. grave
3. sobriety	c. mesmerizing
4. solemn	d. shabby
5. soporific	e. composed
6. sporadic	f. resigned
7. spurious	g. temperance
8. squalid	h. perplexing
9. stagnate	i. vegetate
10. stoic	j. intermittent
	k. fabricated

FILL IN THE BLANK

Use the new words in the following sentences.

1. Trudy was _____ about her musical ability, but she yielded to the argument that she would never really know until she took a few lessons.

2. With the aid of computers, ideas which have been allowed to _____ for ages can be brought up to date and put to use.

3. The _____ follows the theory that what can't be cured must be endured.

4. Raising children to respect honest labor is a _____ responsibility of every parent.

5. The _____ charge by the opposition party did not prevent the president from carrying out his threat of vetoing the bill.

6. Commenting on a person of _____ character, A.B. Evans said, "Beauty's only skin deep, but ugly goes to the bone."

7. Ms. Esposito manages to maintain a _____ atmosphere in her classroom though that is not to say it is a sanctuary of peace and quiet at all times.

8. The speaker's tone and manner exuded a _____ that even the most frivolous minded person could not scoff at.

9. Rosalina was startled out of her _____ mood by the scurrilous attack on her brother.

10. The electric company apologized for the _____ brownouts

but claimed these would not occur if consumers followed the suggestion to cut down on the use of air conditioners during peak hours.

TRUE OR FALSE

Based upon the way the new words are used, identify the following sentences as T (True) or F (False).

1. I find the late night talk shows as soporific as a sleeping pill.

2. The gemologist's appraisal confirmed the value of the spurious diamond broach at $2 million.

3. The squalid furnishings in the posh house made the building a likely prospect for landmark status.

4. After his initial success, the poet's reputation stagnated, and he ultimately was consigned to literary oblivion.

5. Connie's stoic acceptance of her handicap and her determination to live as normal a life as possible made her an admirable role model for others in the hospital.

LESSON 30

■ stringent ■ stultifying ■ substantiate ■ succinct ■ sullen
■ sumptuous ■ supercilious ■ superficial ■ superfluous ■ surmise

stringent *adj.* rigidly controlled or enforced; severe; strict.

The students objected to the *stringent* measures taken by the administration to enforce the dress code.

The army believes that *stringent* training is the best way to assure proper behavior in combat.

The seniors were relieved to hear that the colleges were relaxing their *stringent* requirements for admission.

stultifying *adj.* rendering useless or ineffectual; causing to appear stupid or ridiculous.

It was tragic to observe the venerable politician, having lost his sobriety with his third drink, *stultifying* himself by trying to perform the latest dance.

The soporific effect of the hot sun saved Mr. Stewart from the *stultifying* embarrassment of arguing with the youngsters on the beach over their annoying antics.

The unhappy parents were led to understand that their own lifestyle had a *stultifying* influence on their relationship with their children.

substantiate *v.* to support with proof or evidence; to verify.

The agent told Mr. Perrault he would have to *substantiate* his claim with a receipt before he could be reimbursed for the loss.

It took years to prepare the experiment that would *substantiate* Einstein's Theory of Relativity.

Alice feared that her inability to *substantiate* her charge that she had been unfairly denied promotion would stigmatize her as a troublemaker.

succinct *adj.* clearly expressed in few words; concise; terse.

Shakespeare, the master of the *succinct* phrase, said it best: An honest tale speeds best being plainly told.

Richard, stung by the lateness of the invitation, replied with a *succinct* refusal.

A person who savors action and is *succinct* in speech will not stagnate in a dead-end job.

sullen *adj.* silent and keeping to oneself because one feels angry, bitter or hurt; resentful; morose; sulky.

It takes a stoic disposition to overcome the depressing effect of a *sullen* day.

The wily tyrant feared that in their *sullen* mood the people were ripe for revolt.

When the battle ended, the *sullen* line of soldiers on the losing side retreated to the safety of the hills.

sumptuous *adj.* lavish; costly; extravagantly or luxuriously dressed.

Nathan wanted his wedding to be as *sumptuous* as he could afford.

The campaign opened with a *sumptuous* dinner where high society could be seen rubbing shoulders with aspiring politicians.

The recluse lived in a *sumptuous* mansion into which he had poured millions, but it lacked the human touch of laughter and love.

supercilious *adj.* proud and scornful; haughty; looking down on others.

Upon his appointment to the diplomatic service, Mr. Kinsey became *supercilious* and patronizing, and he quickly lost the popularity that won him the coveted position.

Laurie weathered the *supercilious* sneer of the manager and resolved to file her complaint about his misconduct.

Mr. Barker's *supercilious* manner succeeded only in estranging his friends and winning him the title of "most likely to be fired next."

superficial *adj.* concerned with comprehending what is apparent or obvious; hasty; of or near the surface.

The duel ended with both adversaries sustaining *superficial* wounds.

The cousins bore a *superficial* physical resemblance to each other but they were worlds apart in character.

Dr. Renfold told the class that a *superficial* reading of the poem would not be sufficient to gain an appreciation of its beauty and wisdom.

superfluous *adj.* beyond what is required or sufficient; extra.

Mr. Wallace advised Marilu to tone down all those *superfluous* gestures that she thought were adding dramatic flourishes to her performance.

Kim's remark about her neighbor's obviously overweight son was entirely *superfluous* and quite inconsiderate.

"It is *superfluous* to remind me to drive carefully, Dad," Sean said. "I've already proved to you that I'm not a daredevil when I get behind the wheel."

surmise *v.* to imagine or infer on slight grounds.

We must not *surmise* that gossip has a monopoly on truth.

Sherlock Holmes could *surmise* from the slightest clue a detailed picture of a person's physical characteristics and behavioral traits.

The police tried to calm the mother's fears by telling her that it was rash to *surmise* the worst just because her child was late from school.

SPOTLIGHT ON

supercilious It is characteristic to raise the eyebrows—in Latin, *supercilisus*—to show disdain or haughtiness when one looks down on another. *Supercilious* thus refers to the part of the body used to express arrogance.

succinct What does *succinct* have to do with a girdle? Easy. Just as a succinct expression encircles the thought in a brief phrase, so a girdle encircles the body in as small a space as possible. The Latin *succinctus* means "girdled," and our *cincture*, used mostly poetically, is "a belt or girdle."

MATCHING

Match the words in Column A with their definitions in Column B.

A	B
1. stringent	a. glum
2. stultifying	b. childish
3. substantiate	c. shallow
4. succinct	d. compact
5. sullen	e. magnificent
6. sumptuous	f. rendering absurd
7. supercilious	g. conjecture
8. superficial	h. severe
9. superfluous	i. non-essential
10. surmise	j. arrogant
	k. corroborate

FILL IN THE BLANK

Use the new words in the following sentences.

1. The _____ differences in their backgrounds faded in the warm friendship and camaraderie that developed among the members of the orchestra.

2. Considering their close relationship, Harold's apology seemed _____ but Carmen was genuinely pleased that he had made the effort.

3. In a world filled with uncertainty, we live by what we can _____.

4. Debate continues to rage over the efficacy of _____ laws.

5. Speakers who are not _____ will lose their audience because few people can tolerate rambling and redundancies.

6. Mr. Dillon believed the _____ display of his generosity would earn him acceptance into the 400 Club.

7. The councilman rejected as mere sophistry the spurious argument that the failure to increase taxes was _____ to the effort to attract more business.

8. Phil, far from being discouraged by Marsha's _____ stare, took it as a challenge to prove he could charm her "down to size."

9. "No need to _____ your status as a ghost," said the Count. "I'll just check your sheet number."

10. Masking his _____ disappointment, the defeated candi-

date said a curt farewell to the few loyal party members who remained in the quiet hall.

TRUE OR FALSE

Based upon the way the new words are used, identify whether the following sentences are T (True) or F (False).

1. The teacher assigned a succinct composition of ten pages for the next day.

2. Clara's supercilious interest in everyone's problems conferred on her the status of a den mother.

3. Geraldo thanked us for the superfluous gift, saying it was exactly what he wanted.

4. The sullen, pouting child could not be induced to join the party games.

5. The stringent enforcement of the speed limit was expected to save lives.

REVIEW EXERCISES: LESSONS 26-30

ANALOGIES

Each question below consists of a pair of related words or phrases, followed by five lettered pairs of words or phrases. Select the lettered pair that best expresses a relationship similar to that expressed in the original pair.

1. REBUFF:OFFER::
    (A) relax:pool (B) loosen:knot (C) witness:perjury
    (D) practice:mimic (E) banish:country

2. RAZE:ERECT::
    (A) predict:anticipate (B) respect:revere
    (C) retaliate:forgive (D) modify:correct (E) fidget:fret

3. SAGACIOUS:SAVANT::
    (A) fearless:hero (B) knowledgeable:student
    (C) relative:relation (D) impetuous:terrorist
    (E) tolerant:judge

4. REPUDIATE:RENOUNCE::
    (A) preach:evaluate (B) dominate:harass
    (C) praise:applaud (D) consent:overlook
    (E) perish:disappear

5. SANCTION:LICENSE::
    (A) doctrine:formulate (B) victory:cheer
    (C) possession:acquire (D) rejection:refuse
    (E) sincerity:praise

6. SCOFF:IGNORE::
    (A) fire:hire (B) condemn:disregard
    (C) praise:reject (D) bribe:persuade
    (E) ignite:douse

7. STRINGENT:LAX::
    (A) distracted:solemn (B) dietetic:healthy
    (C) affordable:comfortable (D) romantic:compassionate
    (E) fidgety:composed

8. SPORADIC:SCATTERED::
   - (A) seductive:corrupt   (B) spontaneous:original
   - (C) spectacular:fabulous   (D) hasty:cautious
   - (E) thankful:humble

9. SUMPTUOUS:MEAGER::
   - (A) modest:conceited   (B) melancholy:depressed
   - (C) optimistic:wary   (D) renewable:permanent
   - (E) odd:peculiar

10. SUPERFICIAL:SHALLOW::
   - (A) valuable:overpriced   (B) sincere:doubtful
   - (C) sufficient:adequate   (D) restless:patient
   - (E) puzzling:dazzling

ANTONYMS

Choose the word or phrase that is most nearly *opposite* in meaning to the word in capital letters.

1. RAZE: (A) plant   (B) threaten   (C) increase
   (D) jinx   (E) restore

2. REBUFF: (A) polish   (B) scratch   (C) welcome
   (D) consider   (E) propose

3. RECALCITRANT: (A) harsh   (B) decalcified   (C) diluted
   (D) docile   (E) intriguing

4. RECLUSE: (A) designer   (B) tenant   (C) modernist
   (D) joiner   (E) standard bearer

5. REDUNDANT: (A) concise   (B) foul   (C) sedate
   (D) flavorsome   (E) soluble

6. REFURBISH: (A) deviate   (B) prevent the spread of
   (C) mismatch   (D) allow to deteriorate
   (E) ignore warnings

7. REJUVENATE: (A) forget   (B) grow old   (C) exploit
   (D) plunder   (E) withdraw support from

8. RELEGATE: (A) exile   (B) disobey   (C) violate
   (D) capture   (E) advance

9. RELIC: (A) something expendable   (B) something
   auctionable   (C) anecdote   (D) painting
   (E) token

10. REMORSE: (A) mercy   (B) shamelessness
    (C) aftermath   (D) harmony   (E) merit

HEADLINES

Select the word that fits best in the newspaper headlines below.

1. LAWMAKERS MAKE _____ PRECONDITION FOR LICENSE

    (RELIC, SOBRIETY, RESPITE, REMORSE)

2. MULTIPLE MURDERER EXPRESSES NO _____ FOR CRIMES

    (RESPITE, REBUFF, SANCTION, REMORSE)

3. _____ BEQUEATHES FORTUNE TO PET MONKEY

    (RECLUSE, STOIC, SECTARIAN, RELIC)

4. EXPERTS DISCOUNT _____ EFFECTS OF EXPLOSION

    (SALUTARY, STULTIFYING, SPURIOUS, RESIDUAL)

5. _____ STRIFE SCUTTLES ACCORD

    (RUTHLESS, STRINGENT, SECTARIAN, REDUNDANT)

6. _____ WIFE WON'T TESTIFY AGAINST SPOUSE

    (SOLEMN, RETICENT, REPUGNANT, SQUALID)

7. RESEARCHERS _____ AIDS CURE IS A DECADE AWAY

    (RAZE, RELEGATE, SURMISE, SEQUESTER)

8. SURPRISE WITNESS _____ DEFENDANT'S CLAIM

    (SCOFFS, SUBSTANTIATES, SEQUESTERS, RESCINDS)

9. _____ FIGHTING CONTINUES IN CAPITAL DESPITE TRUCE

    (SUPERFLUOUS, RUTHLESS, SPORADIC, SULLEN)

10. TOY FIRM _____ AT RUMORS OF TAKEOVER

    (RETRACTS, REPUDIATES, RAZES, SCOFFS)

LESSON 31

■ surreptitious ■ susceptible ■ sycophant ■ taciturn ■ tactless
■ talon ■ tangential ■ tawdry ■ tedious ■ temerity

surreptitious *adj.* sly; stealthy; done in a quiet or secret way.

The trouble started with *surreptitious* phone calls to both neighbors that each one surmised came from the other.

The lawyer argued that a *surreptitious* wink is hardly enough to substantiate a claim that there was a bona fide contract.

The *surreptitious* copies of the pamphlet attained a superficial success until they were confiscated by the government.

susceptible *adj.* very sensitive; capable of being acted upon, influenced or affected by a specific trait.

School attendance in the wintertime is likely to be poor because the children are more *susceptible* to colds in that season.

Because she was a very *susceptible* young woman, her parents worried that she might fall into bad company.

The absence of natural barriers made the province *susceptible* to invasion.

sycophant *n.* one who tries to win favor or advance himself by flattering persons of influence; a servile self-seeker.

We can surmise that the *sycophant* will switch loyalties as soon as he is offered a better deal.

The supercilious tyrant surrounded himself with a band of *sycophants*.

The *sycophant* was put in the stultifying position of denigrating the very same policy that he had yesterday embraced.

taciturn *adj.* habitually untalkative; laconic; uncommunicative.

Silas's long years of solitude had made him a *taciturn*, brooding man unused even to the sound of his own voice.

A wise man explained the advantage of being *taciturn* this way: "I have often regretted my speech, never my silence."

144

Leonard's stammering, it is superfluous to say, had much to do with his being so *taciturn* among strangers.

tactless *adj.* not having or showing a sense of the right thing to do or say without causing anger or hurt feelings; without skill in dealing with people.

Bringing up the matter of Grace's losing her job was just about the most *tactless* way to start the conversation.

One way to avoid making a *tactless* remark is to put yourself in the place of the listener.

"I don't wish to be *tactless*," the interviewer said, "but you'll have to give us a more exact age than 21 plus."

talon *n.* the claw of a bird of prey; a human finger or hand that looks or grasps like a claw; any object suggestive of a heel or claw.

The hawk's *talons* closed on its prey, locking it in a vise-like grip.

The wounded bird used its *talons*, its beak, and its wings in a vain effort to escape from the trap.

Dr. Friedrich thought he could discern a rudimentary heel in the prehistoric *talon* that had been unearthed in Tasmania.

tangential *adj.* diverging or digressing; merely touching a subject, not dealing with it at length.

The matter of Eleanor's failure was mentioned at the dinner table only in a *tangential* way, but it hurt her deeply.

The *tangential* approach may be considerate but it wastes much time in coming to grips with the central problem.

Heloise's *tangential* reference to her post-curfew return was enough to set her father's antenna vibrating.

tawdry *adj.* gaudy and cheap; vulgarly ornamental.

Mrs. Pinkerton did not seem to realize her dress was *tawdry* and out of place in the haute couture gathering.

Brightly colored garlands draped the buildings along the parade route in a *tawdry* display of patriotism.

Isabella needed but one glance to rule out the wedding dress as too *tawdry* for her.

tedious *adj.* long or verbose and wearisome; tiresome; boring.

I prefer the fast-paced games of football and basketball to baseball with its *tedious* stretches of waiting for something to happen.

The *tedious* Congressional investigations, with their endless repetitions and concentration on minutiae, soon lost most of their listeners.

Jed felt the *tedious* and embarrassing question by her parents was a small price to pay for the privilege of spending the evening with their daughter.

temerity *n.* rashness; foolish or reckless boldness.

Jack's *temerity* in constantly correcting his superiors cost him his job.

Only the *temerity* of youth could explain Albert's challenge to take on an adversary 50 pounds heavier and five inches taller than he.

With no more than two years of law school to his credit, Richard had the *temerity* to criticize the Chief Justice's decision.

SPOTLIGHT ON

sycophant From the Greek word for "fig shower" or "accuser." Showing a fig or making the sign of a fig was the gesture used to denounce a culprit. The connection to the modern meaning of the word is a warning that friendship bought with favors can quickly turn sour when the flatterer perceives he can profit more from betraying his benefactor than by serving him.

tawdry An example of a mispronunciation that has been upgraded to respectability, *tawdry* was originally St. Audrey's laces, women's neckpieces of a cheap and showy variety sold at St. Audrey's fair in England. The slurring of the initial letter left us with the modern *tawdry*, connoting tastelessly showy clothes.

MATCHING

Match the words in Column A with their definitions in Column B.

A	B
1. surreptitious	a. reticent
2. susceptible	b. clutch
3. sycophant	c. audacity
4. taciturn	d. parasite
5. tactless	e. clandestine
6. talon	f. monotonous
7. tangential	g. sleazy
8. tawdry	h. indiscreet
9. tedious	i. impressionable
10. temerity	j. incidental
	k. martial

FILL IN THE BLANK

Use the new words in the following sentences.

1. To put it succinctly, Edna was too _____ to flattery to protect herself against the unscrupulous lothario.

2. In choosing a date for her _____ friend, Felicia wondered whether to go for gabby Gary or silent Sam.

3. Mr. Furtado was reprimanded for handling the plagiarism issue in such a _____ manner.

4. When Clifford plunged into the raging fire to rescue the screaming children, he may have crossed the thin line between bravery and _____.

5. Felipe sought to capture attention with his _____ jewelry and outlandish clothing.

6. The _____ has neither morals nor pride but cares only for his sumptuous living and undeserved honors.

7. The _____ of an eagle can be as destructive as the claw of a tiger.

8. The interview with the banker, which Bob at first considered a _____ assignment, suddenly became an exciting exploration in the world of finance.

9. The guests cast _____ glances at the clock, hoping the strident music would end shortly.

10. The matter of the salary increases for the officers of the corpora-

tion was included in a _____ note tucked away with the footnotes.

TRUE OR FALSE

Based on the way the new words are used, identify the following sentences as T (True) or F (False).

1. Before the performance, the magician surreptitiously planted her props throughout the auditorium.

2. Jesse's tactless remark boosted his reputation and earned him consideration to write the lead editorial.

3. Don't expect to find anything of quality in the flea market because it seems to concentrate on tawdry merchandise.

4. It was not temerity but arrogance that prompted Melvin to challenge the incumbent.

5. We can consider the major points only after we have dealt with the tangential issues.

Lesson 32

■ tenet ■ tentative ■ terse ■ threadbare ■ thwart ■ tirade
■ trepidation ■ turbulence ■ unassailable ■ undermine

tenet *n.* a principle, doctrine or belief held as a truth by a group.

Most people are not susceptible to deviation from the *tenets* they have been taught in their youth.

It was tactless and presumptuous to ask the official to reveal the secret code and transgress a *tenet* of his profession.

The two theologians differed on whether celibacy was a *tenet* of the faith or merely a tangential belief.

tentative *adj.* made, done or proposed experimentally; not definite or final; indicating timidity, hesitancy, or uncertainty.

Until all the evidence had been gathered, the police could only offer a *tentative* explanation for the explosion.

The plan to exempt low-income families from taxation met with *tentative* Congressional approval.

Climbing to the top of the pole, the aerialist cast a *tentative* glance at the thin wire that would be his pathway across the endless chasm.

terse *adj.* using only a few words but clear and to the point; polished.

The *terse* statement read by the Secretary of State was tantamount to a rejection of the treaty.

A *terse* message surreptitiously delivered to the prisoner in the innocuous birthday card indicated that the escape attempt would be made the following night.

The sycophant, usually effusive in his flattery, became strangely *terse* and ill-humored.

threadbare *adj.* with the nap worn down so that the threads show; frayed or shabby; used so often that it is stale.

The salesman's repertoire of *threadbare* jokes left us wishing he were more taciturn.

The colorful oversized coat, now *threadbare* and torn, hung on the beggar like a tawdry blanket on a scarecrow.

The children, entranced by the raconteur's stirring tale, paid little heed to his *threadbare* clothing.

thwart *v.* to oppose directly; to baffle; to block; to frustrate.

The tight defense was able to *thwart* a touchdown in the last thirty seconds of play.

After she had been turned down five times, Samantha felt some mysterious power was out to *thwart* her hopes of becoming an actress.

The fledgling congressman had the temerity to *thwart* the passage of the bill that the party leader had endorsed.

tirade *n.* a long, angry or scolding speech; a harangue.

With the ferocity of a wild bird sinking its talons into its prey, the senator lambasted his opponent in a *tirade* that left no fault unexposed, no weakness unexploited.

Mr. Cumming's *tirade* was mercifully interrupted by an urgent call from his wife.

I have yet to hear reason and common sense in a speech that degenerates into a *tirade*.

trepidation *n.* a trembling; apprehension; a state of alarm and dread.

The memory of Black Monday has filled investors with *trepidation* about risking more of their money in the stock market.

Noah approached the high trapeze without *trepidation*, confident that the net would save him if he happened to slip.

Sheba was filled with *trepidation* as she waited for her cue to go on stage.

turbulence *n.* violent motion; disorder; excitement.

The captain apologized for the discomfort caused by the *turbulence* in the atmosphere.

The president denied that the changes in the White House staff were evidence of a *turbulence* in his administration.

Concetta's preference for a placid lifestyle can be easily explained as a reaction to the *turbulence* of her early years.

unassailable *adj.* undeniable; unquestionable; not liable to attack.

Brenda's claim that she was exempt from taxation because she had earned no money was *unassailable.*

Thorpe offered an *unassailable* alibi — he was in prison at the time of the crime.

The defenders built a fortress atop the mountain that was virtually *unassailable.*

undermine *v.* to dig or to make a tunnel under; to wear away and weaken the support of; to injure or to weaken in a slow or sneaky way.

The constant pressure of water in the subterranean channels can *undermine* the building's foundation.

Selling below cost will *undermine* the competition, but it will also cause you tremendous losses that you may never recoup.

Ms. Jonas always found something positive to say, for she knew that unrelieved criticism would *undermine* her student's confidence.

SPOTLIGHT ON

turbulence Once you have learned that the meaning of the Latin root *turba* is "confusion or tumult," you can make an intelligent guess at other words with similar etymology: *turbid, turbine,* or *turbo-jet.* You must not assume, however, that *turban* is related since the latter is derived from the Turkish root *tülbent.*

thwart The many variations in the usage of *thwart,* derived from the Old Norse *thvert,* have in common the idea of "across, transverse or oblique." This is apparent in its variant forms; as an adjective meaning "perverse or stubborn"; as a verb, meaning "to oppose, baffle, defeat or block"; and as a noun, meaning "opposition" or "the rower's seat extending across (athwart) a boat."

MATCHING

Match the words in Column A with their definitions in Column B.

<u>A</u>	<u>B</u>
1. tenet	a. chastisement
2. tentative	b. disable
3. terse	c. ragged
4. threadbare	d. violence
5. thwart	e. compact
6. tirade	f. provisional
7. trepidation	g. precept
8. turbulence	h. cheerless
9. unassailable	i. foil
10. undermine	j. impregnable
	k. quaking

FILL IN THE BLANK

Use the new words in the following sentences.

1. Exercising such rigid control over the child's choice of books could _____ his love for reading.

2. The _____ carpet and the shabby furniture were ample proof that the family was living in squalor.

3. Mr. Ruiz refused to go along with the scheme that would have violated the _____ of loyalty he held sacred.

4. For the person lacking confidence, every step is _____.

5. Realizing the enemy forces were _____ on land, General Ramirez decided to blockade the seacoast and starve them into submission.

6. A steady diet of junk food combined with irregular hours can easily _____ a person's health.

7. The student's quickly learned to dismiss Mr. Hall's _____ as an expression of his frustrations.

8. After the frenzy and _____ of a typical business day, Ms. Novick found respite and satisfaction in the pleasure of reading.

9. The brave are not without fear, but they will not let their _____ immobilize them into cowardice.

10. Ms. Lansing advised her students to keep their writing _____ and free of errors.

TRUE OR FALSE

Based on the way the new words are used, identify the following sentences as T (True) or F (False).

1. The union leader ended his thunderous tirade against the company with a call for a strike.

2. The atmosphere in the board room was too charged with passion to risk a turbulent debate.

3. The party unity was undermined with the unstinting approval of the new chairman.

4. Ms. Mendez dismissed the dishonest employee with a terse statement of regret.

5. The faulty design as well as the flimsy construction left the vehicle unassailable.

LESSON 33

■ unequivocal ■ unethical ■ ungainly ■ unimpeachable
■ unobstrusive ■ unscathed ■ untenable ■ urbane ■ utopian
■ vacillate

unequivocal *adj.* plain; very clear in meaning.

Mandy was *unequivocal* in refusing to join the snobbish sorority.

It was political suicide for the congressman to take an *unequivocal* position favoring abortion when so many of his constituents were pro-life.

"Yes," said the prime minister to the UN chief, "but what assurance is there the world body will back up its *unequivocal* guarantee?"

unethical *adj.* not conforming to approved standards of behavior, a socially accepted code, or professionaly endorsed principles and practices.

It is no longer considered *unethical* or uncouth for a lawyer to advertise his or her services.

The *unethical* behavior of so many of the governor's appointees undermined his reputation and placed his reelection in jeopardy.

Many victims of cancer willl turn to *unethical* charlatans in a desperate search for a cure.

ungainly *adj.* clumsy; awkward; hard to handle.

Geraldo's sensitivity about his threadbare garments made him *ungainly*.

Elsie's curtsy was so *ungainly* it is a wonder she did not lose her balance and topple over.

As she struggled to poke her head through the tuba, Terry wondered, "Why on earth did I choose such an *ungainly* instrument?"

unimpeachable *adj.* beyond doubt or reproach; unquestionable.

Hector has always been known for his *unimpeachable* honesty.

The newspaperman stood by his story, insisting he had obtained his information from an *unimpeachable* source.

154

Until his indictment for income tax evasion, the chairman of the board had enjoyed an *unimpeachable* reputation.

unobtrusive *adj.* not readily noticeable; inconspicuous.

Mr. Cottrell's *unobtrusive* demeanor was a perfect front for his undercover work.

Filled with trepidation, Charlotte tried to make her late entrance as *unobtrusive* as possible.

Paul's friends, accustomed to his *unobtrusive* manner, could not imagine what had brought on his turbulent outbreak.

unscathed *adj.* undamaged; unharmed.

Ethan was delighted to have gotten through the first two interviews *unscathed*.

Rebecca came through her freshman year with her reputation as a straight A student *unscathed*.

Theseus was not thwarted by the warning that no one ever returned from the cave of the Minotaur *unscathed*.

untenable *adj.* that which cannot be maintained or occupied; incapable of being defended or held.

The lack of heat and hot water made the apartment *untenable*.

Keith persisted in his alibi although it was obviously *untenable*.

The captain did not give the order to retreat even when the position became *untenable*.

urbane *adj.* courteous; suave; polished.

Mr. Darcy's *urbane* manner immediately attracted Mrs. Bennett's attention.

Nancy maintained an *urbane* tone in her correspondence with Ira, never overstepping the bounds of propriety.

What is remarkable about Consuelo is that she retains her *urbane* posture no matter how distressed she is.

utopian *adj.* excellent, but existing only in fancy or theory; given to dreams or schemes of perfection.

The UN has not fulfilled the *utopian* dreams of its founders.

Whenever we hear promises of *utopian* panaceas, we can assume that the speaker is on a visit to earth from his castle in the air.

Civilization has profited from *utopian* plans, for they often guide us to a better future.

vacillate *v.* to sway unsteadily; to totter; to waver; to fluctuate.

Brian's tendency to *vacillate* makes him a poor choice for president.

In choosing a mate, we *vacillate* between concentrating on one characteristic or another, but we don't take the plunge until someone with the right combination comes along.

The adage about not changing horses in midstream suggests that one should not *vacillate* once a decision has been made.

SPOTLIGHT ON

urbane Country folk were once considered coarse or crude because education was not readily available to them. But as the word *urbane* suggests, the city slickers did not fare much better, for they were credited with the possession not of substantial knowledge but of superficial social graces.

utopian Utopia is an imaginary island described in Sir Thomas Moore's *Utopia* (1516), a place of ideal laws and social conditions. Significantly, the Greek words *on*, "no", and *topos*, "country," tell us that the author realized this state of perfection was unattainable. However, it is worthwhile to have a target at which to aim.

MATCHING

Match the words in Column A with their definitions in Column B.

A	B
1. unequivocal	a. intact
2. unethical	b. irreproachable
3. ungainly	c. cultivated
4. unimpeachable	d. indefensible
5. unobtrusive	e. unassuming
6. unscathed	f. unambiguous
7. untenable	g. hesitate
8. urbane	h. clumsy
9. utopian	i. dishonest
10. vacillate	j. impure
	k. idealistic

FILL IN THE BLANK

Use the new words in the following sentences.

1. Miraculously the entire family emerged _____ from the accident, but the car was totally wrecked.

2. Malcolm was advised by his counsel to plead guilty, for his claim to have been under the influence of an alien being was _____.

3. Phyllis had a _____ outlook while her husband was eminently practical, but they seldom argued because they seemed to be living in two different worlds.

4. No _____ apology could still the turbulence in Kevin's heart over the insult.

5. The upshot of the investigation was that Mr. Callan could not be prosecuted for illegal behavior, but there was little doubt that what he did was _____.

6. Two short years have transformed Alicia from a shy, _____ adolescent into an exquisite young lady.

7. Until his senior year, Wayne continued to _____ between engineering and advertising as a career.

8. Mr. Talbot launched into a tirade of slander against the man he had until now considered _____.

9. Mr. Simmons made an _____ promise to his wife that he would stop gambling.

10. Banging on his door at three in the morning was hardly an _____ way to gain admittance.

TRUE OR FALSE

Based on the way the new words are used, identify the following sentences as T (True) or F (False).

1. The ungainly child, primarily because of his grace and charm, became a box office star.

2. Perry did not hide his disappointment with Roderick's unethical behavior in revealing their private conversations.

3. The wounded knight clanked unobtrusively over the moat and demanded asylum.

4. Mr. Foster ended his vacillation by declaring resolutely, "Give me a month or so and I will try to come up with a decision, if I am able."

5. Lonnie was physically unscathed in the brief encounter but his ego was badly bruised.

LESSON 34

validate *v.* to declare or make legally sound; to substantiate; to verify.

> Floyd said he had an unimpeachable witness to *validate* his claims.

> The summit produced a treaty which the Senate must now *validate.*

> I cannot *validate* these foreign documents since I do not understand the language.

venerate *v.* to regard with respect and reverence; to honor.

> One way to *venerate* our parents is to emulate their deeds.

> We *venerate* others for their achievements rather than for their possessions.

> Is it a utopian wish that our children will venerate us just as we *venerate* our parents?

verbose *adj.* wordy; tedious.

> Craig mistakenly believed that being urbane meant being *verbose.*

> When the *verbose* speaker stopped to take a drink of water, Cheryl unobtrusively slipped out of the auditorium.

> Roy had two faults: he was *verbose* and he was ungainly, a combination that was not designed to win him friends.

viable *adj.* able to live or exist; practicable.

> Professor Fields agreed to accept a diary as a *viable* substitute for a short story.

> Laverne admitted that a blind date was a *viable* alternative to a forlorn evening alone.

> The stranded mountain climbers looked for *viable* living arrangements until help arrived.

vicarious *adj.* taking the place of another; experienced through sympathetic participation in the experience of another.

The *vicarious* thrill we get from watching films falls short of the pleasure of first hand experience.

Mr. Scully derived a *vicarious* pleasure from seeing the children squeal with delight as they watched the circus performers.

The class did not take kindly to Ms. Corfu's imposing *vicarious* punishment just because she felt she had to teach somebody a lesson.

vilify *v.* to defame; to slander; to cause a person to become vile.

The general refused to *vilify* his subordinates and accepted the onus of the defeat himself.

The unscrupulous candidate withdrew from the race when his attempt to *vilify* his opponent backfired.

Beverly said nothing could induce her to *vilify* someone she knew to be upright.

vindictive *adj.* revengeful; unforgiving; bitter; spiteful.

We were relieved that Emily was not *vindictive* about our having made her the butt of an uncouth joke.

The surprise test seemed to be a *vindictive* act on Mr. Rollin's part to punish us for mistreating the substitute the day before.

The terrorists' *vindictive* attack on a pleasure boat was indignantly condemned by the international community.

virtuoso *n.* one interested in the pursuit of knowledge; one with masterly skill or technique in any field, as in the arts.

Even at an early age Carico showed the promise that would one day blossom into the talents of a piano *virtuoso*.

No *virtuoso* could have performed that concerto with greater finesse and skill than Marian.

Lena's love of learning and the patience to acquire it presage her emergence as a *virtuoso* in the field of chemistry, which she chose as her career.

vitriolic *adj.* extremely biting or caustic; sharp and bitter.

Such *vitriolic* talk will not help to reconcile the feuding parties.

The deposed chairman poured all his hatred into the *vitriolic* speech.

A mere mention of the enemy would bring on a *vitriolic* tirade.

volatile *adj.* evaporating readily at normal temperatures; change-able; explosive; lighthearted; fleeting.

Alcohol and ether are highly *volatile* substances.

Court-ordered busing has generated a *volatile* political atmosphere.

The escaping gas created a *volatile* condition that had to be dealt with immediately.

SPOTLIGHT ON

vicarious The word *vicar*, which occurs in *vicarious*, derives from the Latin *vicarius*, which means "substitute" or "deputy." A vicar, in fact, is considered by the church as a representative or agent of God on earth.

vitriolic In chemistry, vitriol is sulfuric acid, a highly corrosive substance which can burn and cause serious injury. Applied to speech, the word refers to language that can have a searing effect on someone's feelings.

MATCHING

Match the words in Column A with their definitions in Column B.

A	B
1. validate	a. revengeful
2. venerate	b. caustic
3. verbose	c. celibate
4. viable	d. long-winded
5. vicarious	e. certify
6. vilify	f. malign
7. vindictive	g. workable
8. virtuoso	h. esteem
9. vitriolic	i. acting as a substitute
10. volatile	j. unstable
	k. connoisseur

FILL IN THE BLANK

Use the new words in the following sentences.

1. Politicians have a reputation for being _____ and that is strange for that will hardly endear them to their audience.

2. Unwilling to tolerate the official's vacillation, Arnold asked him to either _____ or return his papers.

3. Mr. Stone considered his offer to join the firm as a _____ means of avoiding bankruptcy, but having heard some of his untenable ideas, we responded with an unequivocal no.

4. Nothing can so _____ a person as pride and greed.

5. After listening to her daughter perform at the musicale, Mrs. Osborne admitted, "A _____ she is not, but she likes to play and I like to listen to her."

6. Basil's _____ nature was easily recognizable in every line of his poison pen letter.

7. Bob had maintained an amiable tone until Carl unleashed a totally unexpected _____ attack on him.

8. Selma had such a highly developed sense of honesty that she found it impossible to _____ someone who was in the least bit unethical.

9. Tom's _____ mood swings left us wondering if he was not suffering from a chemical imbalance.

10. The _____ pain of his son's injury did not leave Mr. Otis unscathed, for many days passed before that grim picture faded from his memory.

TRUE OR FALSE

Based on the way the new words are used, identify the following sentences as T (True) or F (False).

1. Vicarious experiences form a substantial part of our store of knowledge.

2. The vitriolic application soothed the festering sore.

3. The volatile liquid, dangerous at normal temperatures, posed no immediate threat of explosion.

4. Though many viable suggestions were offered, not one was accepted at the lengthy, inconclusive meeting.

5. Dr. Kroll vilified his home by adding two spacious wings and surrounding the entire structure with elaborate greenery.

LESSON 35

■voluminous ■voracious ■waive ■wanton ■whet ■wither
■writhe ■zany ■zealot ■zenith

---

voluminous *adj.* large, bulky; enough to fill volumes.

Dickens' *voluminous* writings fill many library shelves.

Carla's role required her to wear a *voluminous* dress in which she had to hide certain props.

The senator was given to making *voluminous* speeches, most of which were readily forgotten.

voracious *adj.* ravenous; greedy; gluttonous.

Since her junior year, Susan has been a *voracious* reader.

Carl's *voracious* appetite for chocolate was not satisfied until he had consumed the entire devil's food cake along with an indeterminate amount of candy bars.

The *voracious* guest finally departed, leaving the refrigerator and pantry sadly depleted.

waive *v.* to dispense with; to relinquish; to postpone.

The defense attorney decided to *waive* his right to cross-examine the witness.

The quarterback's decision to *waive* the penalty may have cost us the game.

No citizen should *waive* his right of free speech.

wanton *adj.* immoral; senseless; deliberately malicious; excessive.

The partisans condemned the dictator's *wanton* disregard for human rights.

Peggy's *wanton* behavior brought shame to her family and surprised her friends.

The *wanton* destruction of European Jewry by the Nazis was the worst holocaust in history.

whet *v.* to sharpen; to make stronger; to stimulate.

If you *whet* the blade on this grindstone, you will have a more useful tool to work with.

I was warned that telling Marge one secret would only *whet* her appetite for more.

Drinking soda in the summer tends to *whet* my thirst but fails to cool me off.

wither *v.* to dry up; to shrivel; to cause to lose courage or to be ashamed.

A prolonged drought could *wither* the crops and throw the economy into a tailspin.

Marion knew the flower would *wither* and lose its fragrance, but she still kept it as a memento of her prom.

Mr. Rangel could *wither* an employee with just a glance and so discouraged any friendly overtures from the staff.

writhe *v.* to twist or squirm, as in pain; to suffer from shame or shyness.

When the parents saw the child *writhe* in pain, they decided to rush him to the hospital.

The mere mention of his adversary caused the defeated warrior to *writhe* in anguish.

We watched the wounded snake *writhe* and slither behind a tree, eventually disappearing into a thicket.

zany *adj.* clownish; foolish; funny; absurd.

In hindsight, Karen admitted her *zany* antics had no place in the classroom.

Because of his tendency to make a joke of even a serious matter, Burton gained a reputation as a *zany* young man.

The play had its *zany* turns but underneath it all was Puck's philosophical comment: "What fools these mortals be."

zealot *n.* a person who shows great enthusiasm for a cause.

A *zealot* for political reform will go to almost any lengths to further his cause.

With the faith of a *zealot*, Francine plunged into the battle for women's rights, vowing no letup until victory was in her grasp.

If Adrienne does not gain a place on the Olympic team, it will not be because she lacked the dedication of a *zealot*.

zenith *n.* the point in the sky directly above one; the highest point.

At noon the sun is at its *zenith*.

The tragedy is that Penny was stricken at the *zenith* of her career.

The literary world has yet to decide when Shakespeare reached the *zenith* of his powers.

SPOTLIGHT ON

writhe This word dates back to an Old English word, *writhan*, which has a number of cousins whose close relationship gives us a clue to their meanings. Among these are *wreath*, a twisted band of leaves or flowers, and *wry*, twisted or distorted (as a face or expression).

zany *Zany* is derived from the Italian, *Zanni*, a nickname for *Giovanni*, John. *Zanni* was the name of a stock character in comedies whose role was to clownishly ape the principal character.

MATCHING

Match the words in Column A with their definitions in Column B.

A	B
1. voluminous	a. defer
2. voracious	b. crazy
3. waive	c. squirm
4. wanton	d. insatiable
5. whet	e. apex
6. wither	f. ample
7. writhe	g. reckless
8. zany	h. inflame
9. zealot	i. enthusiast
10. zenith	j. suppress
	k. deteriorate

FILL IN THE BLANK

Use the new words in the following sentences.

1. In an emergency we may have to _____ certain democratic privileges.

2. Father threatened to stop Mark's allowance if he did not change his _____, drunken ways.

3. One could not have guessed, looking at her diminutive size, what a _____ eater she was.

4. From our vantage point we could see the rabbit _____ in the jaws of the cat.

5. The cycle of life continues with all living things: they are born, they blossom and they _____.

6. Without the inspiration of a _____, many great ideas would have died aborning.

7. Few people ever attain the _____ of their aspirations.

8. The annual budget was spelled out in detail in the _____ book the president sent to Congress.

9. Ted's actions may have appeared _____, but as we later learned "there was method to his madness."

10. The movie critic told us just enough to _____ our curiosity, but of course he would not reveal the surprise ending.

TRUE OR FALSE

Based on the way the words are used, identify the following sentences as T (True) or F (False).

1. The little boy had been suffering from a voracious appetite since he lost his two front teeth.

2. The patriot waived the outlawed flag in a defiant gesture.

3. The fiasco brought Rita to the zenith of her career, but she refused to give up because there was nowhere to go but up.

4. Paula admitted that her running away from her responsibilities was a wanton act of self-indulgence.

5. Withering the shock of triple gravity was only the first of many trials for the space travelers.

REVIEW EXERCISES: LESSONS 31-35

ANALOGIES

Each question below consists of a pair of related words or phrases, followed by five lettered pairs of words or phrases. Select the lettered pair that best expresses a relationship similar to that expressed in the original pair.

1. TERSE:VERBOSE::
   (A) wealthy:gaudy (B) astonishing:incredible
   (C) fastidious:sloppy (D) garrulous:gratuitous
   (E) forlorn:unhappy

2. TALON:RIPS::
   (A) sword:duels (B) bullet:pierces (C) ball:flies
   (D) log:rolls (E) bomb:drops

3. THWART:PLAN::
   (A) impeach:president (B) expedite:negotiations
   (C) refuse:bribe (D) claim:victory (E) block:play

4. TREPIDATION:TREMBLE::
   (A) love:romanticize (B) anger:argue
   (C) nervousness:hallucinate (D) amazement:gape
   (E) disaster:hope

5. UNETHICAL:UNSCRUPULOUS::
   (A) fearless:courageous (B) hostile:neighborly
   (C) hospitable:snobbish (D) complimentary:jealous
   (E) quarrelsome:diabolic

6. UTOPIAN:GARDEN OF EDEN::
   (A) military:Pentagon (B) executive:White House
   (C) childish:Disney World (D) idyllic:paradise
   (E) realistic:Hollywood

7. VILIFY:HONOR::
   (A) betray:cheat (B) fascinate:charm
   (C) mold:form (D) differ:compromise (E) insult:flatter

8. VENERATE:HERO::
   (A) fail:math (B) break:law (C) condemn:criminal
   (D) capture:prize (E) preach:sermon

9. WHET:APPETITE::
    (A) stimulate:mind (B) pedal:bicycle (C) launch:boat
    (D) compete:rival (E) confide:suspicion

10. VOLUMINOUS:DIMINUTIVE::
    (A) opposed:antagonistic (B) conscious:wary
    (C) preceding:following (D) slanderous:defamatory
    (E) bewildered:frank

ANTONYMS

Choose the word or phrase that is most nearly *opposite* in meaning to the word in capital letters.

1. SURREPTITIOUS: (A) benevolent (B) brazen
    (C) unique (D) flawless (E) rare

2. SUSCEPTIBLE: (A) gullible (B) flexible (C) hypothetical
    (D) immune (E) impartial

3. TENTATIVE: (A) amended (B) fixed (C) dignified
    (D) antiquated (E) extensive

4. THREADBARE: (A) new (B) graceful (C) inventive
    (D) fashionable (E) generous

5. UNEQUIVOCAL: (A) critical (B) fundamental
    (C) articulate (D) unanimous
    (E) dubious

6. UNOBTRUSIVE: (A) ambiguous (B) persistent
    (C) flamboyant (D) devious (E) tidy

7. VALIDATE: (A) disallow (B) manipulate
    (C) abandon (D) downgrade
    (E) disappear

8. VITRIOLIC: (A) overpowering (B) permissive
    (C) petty (D) cordial (E) mutual

9. VOLUMINOUS: (A) boisterous (B) blank
    (C) pocket-sized (D) unauthorized
    (E) unpublished

10. ZENITH: (A) sage (B) corollary (C) torment
    (D) nadir (E) decline

HEADLINES

Select the word that fits best in the newspaper headlines below.

1. STUDY FINDS ASIANS MORE _____ TO WESTERN DISEASES

   (VICARIOUS, VORACIOUS, TAWDRY, SUSCEPTIBLE)

2. _____ CLAUSE INVALIDATES CONTRACT

   (SURREPTITIOUS, ZANY, VITRIOLIC, UNGAINLY)

3. CHURCH COUNCIL DEBATES MODIFICATION OF BASIC _____

   (ZEALOT, TIRADE, TENET, ZENITH)

4. _____ REFORMER TOUTED FOR VACANT SENATE SEAT

   (UTOPIAN, TACITURN, WANTON, VOLUMINOUS)

5. CONGRESSIONAL AIDE RESIGNS AMID CHARGES OF _____ CONDUCT

   (VIABLE, UNASSAILABLE, VOLATILE, UNETHICAL)

6. CRITICS ACCLAIM _____ PERFORMANCE

   (TERSE, VIRTUOSO, UNEQUIVOCAL, URBANE)

7. CROPS _____ AS DROUGHT CONTINUES

   (WAIVE, UNDERMINE, WITHER, VACILLATE)

8. _____ COMMUNIQUE ANNOUNCES END OF 8-YEAR WAR

   (TERSE, TAWDRY, VINDICTIVE, UNTENABLE)

9. AUTHORITIES STYMIED BY _____ MARKS ON PRISONER'S BODY

   (VICARIOUS, URBANE, UNOBTRUSIVE, TALON)

10. ASTRONAUTS' 6-MONTH EXPEDITION PROVES LIFE IN SPACE IS _____

   (TANGENTIAL, VIABLE, VOLATILE, THREADBARE)

ANSWERS TO EXERCISES

Lesson 1

MATCHING
1. c   2. e   3. h   4. k   5. j   6. a   7. g   8. i   9. f   10. b

FILL IN THE BLANK
1. affinity 2. admonish 3. aberration 4. abstract 5. acquiesce 6. acclaim
7. abstinence 8. advocate 9. aggrandizement 10. aesthetic

TRUE OR FALSE
1. T   2. T   3. F   4. T   5. T

Lesson 2

MATCHING
1. d   2. k   3. f   4. a   5. b   6. h   7. c   8. i   9. j   10. g

FILL IN THE BLANK
1. ambivalence 2. anonymity 3. alienate 4. aloof 5. analogous 6. altruistic
7. animosity 8. ambiguous 9. alleviate 10. ameliorate

TRUE OR FALSE
1. T   2. F   3. T   4. T   5. T

Lesson 3

MATCHING
1. j   2. b   3. e   4. h   5. k   6. a   7. c   8. d   9. f   10. g

FILL IN THE BLANK
1. atrophy 2. assuage 3. authoritarian 4. austere 5. antagonism
6. apochryphal 7. antithesis 8. arduous 9. augment 10. articulate

TRUE OR FALSE
1. T   2. F   3. T   4. T   5. F

Lesson 4

MATCHING
1. d   2. i   3. k   4. c   5. f   6. b   7. g   8. e   9. j   10. h

FILL IN THE BLANK
1. cache 2. autonomy 3. aversion 4. bombastic 5. belittle 6. bizarre
7. buffoon 8. cacophony 9. blithe 10. bequeath

TRUE OR FALSE
1. F   2. T   3. T   4. T   5. T

Lesson 5

MATCHING

1. k 2. i 3. g 4. e 5. b 6. f 7. d 8. h 9. c 10. a

FILL IN THE BLANK

1. celestial 2. carping 3. catalyst 4. caustic 5. censure 6. cajole
7. capitulate 8. capricious 9. callous 10. catharsis

TRUE OR FALSE

1. F 2. T 3. T 4. T 5. T

Review (Lessons 1-5)

ANALOGIES

1. E 2. B 3. A 4. C 5. E 6. C 7. C 8. D 9. A 10. B

ANTONYMS

1. B 2. B 3. D 4. E 5. D 6. A 7. A 8. C 9. B 10. A

HEADLINES

1. bequeath 2. caustic 3. affinity 4. capitulate 5. autonomy 6. callous
7. bizarre 8. alleviate 9. augment 10. capricious

Lesson 6

MATCHING

1. e 2. h 3. c 4. f 5. k 6. g 7. a 8. j 9. i 10. b

FILL IN THE BLANK

1. chimerical 2. clairvoyant 3. clandestine 4. clemency 5. commiserate
6. chastise 7. circumspect 8. chronic 9. colloquial 10. coalesce

TRUE OR FALSE

1. F 2. T 3. T 4. T 5. F

Lesson 7

MATCHING

1. j 2. a 3. k 4. d 5. f 6. h 7. i 8. e 9. g 10. c

FILL IN THE BLANK

1. crass 2. compatible 3. criterion 4. composure 5. conspicuous
6. corroborate 7. concise 8. conciliatory 9. copious 10. condone

TRUE OR FALSE

1. T 2. F 3. T 4. T 5. F

Lesson 8

MATCHING

1. g 2. a 3. b 4. c 5. i 6. k 7. e 8. h 9. f 10. d

FILL IN THE BLANK
1. delineate 2. deflate 3. denunciation 4. cryptic 5. demeanor 6. dearth
7. cursory 8. decadence 9. debilitate 10. deference

TRUE OR FALSE
1. F 2. T 3. T 4. T 5. F

Lesson 9

MATCHING
1. g 2. e 3. f 4. a 5. j 6. b 7. d 8. i 9. c 10. k

FILL IN THE BLANK
1. despot 2. didactic 3. deprecate 4. devious 5. deter 6. desecrate
7. derogatory 8. diffuse 9. devoid 10. diatribe

TRUE OR FALSE
1. T 2. T 3. T 4. T 5. T

Lesson 10

MATCHING
1. k 2. b 3. a 4. i 5. g 6. d 7. c 8. j 9. f 10. h

FILL IN THE BLANK
1. discerning 2. diminution 3. distraught 4. disparity 5. disdain
6. dissipated 7. disposition 8. disperse 9. disparage 10. dismantle

TRUE OR FALSE
1. F 2. T 3. T 4. T 5. F

Review (Lessons 6-10)

ANALOGIES
1. A 2. C 3. C 4. E 5. C 6. A 7. E 8. A 9. B 10. E

ANTONYMS
1. B 2. D 3. A 4. E 5. A 6. B 7. C 8. A 9. C 10. E

HEADLINES
1. clemency 2. chastise 3. disperse 4. decadence 5. chronic 6. diminution
7. distraught 8. corroborate 9. compatible 10. delineate

Lesson 11

MATCHING
1. e 2. b 3. k 4. d 5. a 6. j 7. h 8. g 9. f 10. c

FILL IN THE BLANK
1. eclectic 2. elucidate 3. duplicity 4. egregious 5. ebb 6. elusive 7. efface
8. dogmatic 9. dormant 10. effervescent

TRUE OR FALSE
1. T 2. F 3. T 4. T 5. T

Lesson 12
MATCHING
1. b 2. a 3. k 4. h 5. d 6. e 7. f 8. i 9. j 10. g

FILL IN THE BLANK
1. equivocate 2. equanimity 3. ephemeral 4. embellish 5. engender
6. emulate 7. embroil 8. enigma 9. enhance 10. enervate

TRUE OR FALSE
1. T 2. F 3. T 4. T 5. T

Lesson 13
MATCHING
1. h 2. k 3. a 4. d 5. b 6. f 7. c 8. g 9. e 10. i

FILL IN THE BLANK
1. expedient 2. expunge 3. extol 4. esoteric 5. evanescent 6. exacerbate
7. eulogy 8. exemplary 9. expedite 10. euphemism

TRUE OR FALSE
1. T 2. T 3. T 4. T 5. F

Lesson 14
MATCHING
1. d 2. a 3. j 4. g 5. b 6. h 7. e 8. k 9. f 10. i

FILL IN THE BLANK
1. formidable 2. fallacy 3. fastidious 4. fervor 5. fitful 6. facilitate
7. fledgling 8. fortuitous 9. forlorn 10. flagrant

TRUE OR FALSE
1. T 2. T 3. T 4. T 5. T

Lesson 15
MATCHING
1. k 2. e 3. a 4. d 5. b 6. g 7. i 8. j 9. f 10. h

FILL IN THE BLANK
1. furtive 2. galvanize 3. gullible 4. guile 5. garner 6. haphazard
7. garrulous 8. gratuitous 9. garbled 10. hackneyed

TRUE OR FALSE
1. T 2. F 3. T 4. T 5. F

Review (Lessons 11-15)

ANALOGIES
1. E 2. A 3. B 4. C 5. D 6. A 7. A 8. C 9. C 10. D

ANTONYMS
1. B 2. D 3. A 4. E 5. B 6. A 7. A 8. A 9. C 10. E

HEADLINES
1. dormant 2. exemplary 3. equivocate 4. gratuitous 5. formidable
6. equanimity 7. garner 8. egregious 9. fitful 10. dogmatic

Lesson 16

MATCHING
1. d 2. h 3. f 4. a 5. e 6. k 7. b 8. c 9. j 10. g

FILL IN THE BLANK
1. hypocritical 2. hedonist 3. heretic 4. immaterial 5. imminent
6. iconoclast 7. homogeneous 8. hyperbole 9. hypothetical 10. hierarchy

TRUE OR FALSE
1. T 2. F 3. T 4. T 5. T

Lesson 17

MATCHING
1. i 2. c 3. a 4. b 5. e 6. d 7. k 8. h 9. g 10. f

FILL IN THE BLANK
1. incongruous 2. incontrovertible 3. incipient 4. impartial 5. immutable
6. incisive 7. inadvertent 8. implausible 9. imperturbable 10. impassive

TRUE OR FALSE
1. F 2. T 3. T 4. T 5. T

Lesson 18

MATCHING
1. j 2. h 3. a 4. b 5. k 6. f 7. d 8. e 9. i 10. g

FILL IN THE BLANK
1. incorrigible 2. inscrutable 3. indefatigable 4. intemperate 5. intractable
6. innocuous 7. insurgent 8. ingratiate 9. indigent 10. insipid

TRUE OR FALSE
1. T 2. F 3. T 4. T 5. T

Lesson 19

MATCHING
1. e 2. i 3. g 4. c 5. k 6. f 7. a 8. h 9. b 10. j

FILL IN THE BLANK
1. laconic 2. lampoon 3. kindled 4. lassitude 5. irrefutable 6. jargon
7. labyrinth 8. irrelevant 9. lackluster 10. judicious

TRUE OR FALSE
1. F 2. F 3. T 4. T 5. F

Lesson 20

MATCHING
1. c 2. h 3. a or g 4. k 5. a or g 6. f 7. e 8. i 9. b 10. d

FILL IN THE BLANK
1. lethargic or listless 2. laudable 3. malicious 4. lucid 5. latent
6. meandering 7. marred 8. levity 9. listless or lethargic 10. meager

TRUE OR FALSE
1. F 2. T 3. F 4. F 5. T

Review (Lessons 16-20)

ANALOGIES
1. C 2. D 3. A 4. D 5. B 6. B 7. C 8. E 9. B 10. E

ANTONYMS
1. D 2. C 3. E 4. B 5. C 6. A 7. B 8. B 9. A 10. D

HEADLINES
1. judicious 2. lampoon 3. hedonist 4. imminent 5. imperturbable
6. insipid 7. marred 8. jargon 9. inscrutable 10. incorrigible

Lesson 21

MATCHING
1. d 2. h 3. f 4. j 5. a 6. i 7. c 8. b 9. k 10. g

FILL IN THE BLANK
1. nomenclature 2. obliterate 3. meticulous 4. morose 5. opportunist
6. officious 7. mitigate 8. nonchalance 9. obscure 10. obsolete

TRUE OR FALSE
1. T 2. T 3. F 4. T 5. F

Lesson 22

MATCHING
1. e 2. b 3. g 4. i 5. c 6. j 7. a 8. k 9. h 10. f

FILL IN THE BLANK
1. pariah 2. partisan 3. paucity 4. perceptive 5. peerless 6. opulence
7. perfidy 8. overt 9. parsimonious 10. painstaking

TRUE OR FALSE
1. F 2. T 3. F 4. T 5. T

Lesson 23

MATCHING
1. d 2. j 3. g 4. a 5. f 6. h 7. b 8. k 9. e 10. i

FILL IN THE BLANK
1. pique 2. placate 3. philistine 4. peruse 5. plagiarize 6. pompous
7. peripheral 8. platitude 9. placid 10. piety

TRUE OR FALSE
1. F 2. T 3. T 4. F 5. F

Lesson 24

MATCHING
1. c 2. h 3. k 4. i 5. e 6. g 7. b 8. j 9. a 10. f

FILL IN THE BLANK
1. pragmatic 2. profane 3. ponderous 4. prestigious 5. preclude
6. precocious 7. pretentious 8. ponderous 9. procrastinate 10. profusion

TRUE OR FALSE
1. F 2. T 3. T 4. F 5. T

Lesson 25

MATCHING
1. b 2. i 3. d 4. k 5. j 6. a 7. g 8. e 9. f 10. h

FILL IN THE BLANK
1. querulous 2. quixotic 3. raconteur 4. quandary 5. provincial
6. pugnacious 7. rancor 8. prolific 9. prudent 10. propensity

TRUE OR FALSE
1. T 2. T 3. F 4. T 5. T

Review (Lessons 21-25)

ANALOGIES
1. C 2. B 3. A 4. E 5. A 6. C 7. D 8. B 9. E 10. D

ANTONYMS
1. D 2. E 3. A 4. C 5. C 6. E 7. D 8. B 9. B 10. D

HEADLINES
1. obsolete 2. ponderous 3. peerless 4. perusing 5. morose 6. paucity
7. perfidy 8. precludes 9. prudent 10. pique

Lesson 26

MATCHING
1. d 2. h 3. f 4. b 5. i 6. a 7. k 8. c 9. j 10. g

FILL IN THE BLANK
1. recluse 2. redundant 3. rejuvenate 4. remorse 5. relegate 6. raze
7. refurbish 8. rebuff 9. relic 10. recalcitrant

TRUE OR FALSE
1. F 2. T 3. T 4. F 5. F

Lesson 27

MATCHING
1. j 2. e 3. g 4. a 5. d 6. c 7. i 8. b 9. k 10. h

FILL IN THE BLANK
1. residual 2. resilient 3. repudiate 4. rescind 5. repugnant 6. retract
7. reticent 8. ruthless 9. sagacious 10. respite

TRUE OR FALSE
1. F 2. F 3. F 4. T 5. T

Lesson 28

MATCHING
1. h 2. d 3. a 4. f 5. j 6. k 7. e 8. b 9. g 10. c

FILL IN THE BLANK
1. savory 2. sanction 3. sequester 4. saturate 5. scoff 6. scapegoat
7. scrutinize 8. scrupulous 9. sectarian 10. salutary

TRUE OR FALSE
1. T 2. F 3. T 4. T 5. F

Lesson 29

MATCHING
1. e 2. a 3. g 4. b 5. c 6. j 7. k 8. d 9. i 10. f

FILL IN THE BLANK
1. skeptical 2. stagnate 3. stoic 4. solemn 5. spurious 6. squalid 7. serene
8. sobriety 9. soporific 10. sporadic

TRUE OR FALSE
1. T 2. F 3. F 4. T 5. T

Lesson 30

MATCHING
1. h 2. f 3. k 4. d 5. a 6. e 7. j 8. c 9. i 10. g

FILL IN THE BLANK
1. superficial 2. superfluous 3. surmise 4. stringent 5. succinct
6. sumptuous 7. stultifying 8. supercilious 9. substantiate 10. sullen

TRUE OR FALSE
1. F 2. F 3. F 4. T 5. T

Review (Lessons 26-30)

ANALOGIES
1. B 2. C 3. A 4. C 5. D 6. B 7. E 8. C 9. A 10. C

ANTONYMS
1. E 2. C 3. D 4. D 5. A 6. D 7. B 8. E 9. A 10. B

HEADLINES
1. sobriety 2. remorse 3. recluse 4. residual 5. sectarian 6. reticent
7. surmise 8. substantiates 9. sporadic 10. scoffs

Lesson 31

MATCHING
1. e 2. i 3. d 4. a 5. h 6. b 7. j 8. g 9. f 10. c

FILL IN THE BLANK
1. susceptible 2. taciturn 3. tactless 4. temerity 5. tawdry 6. sycophant
7. talon 8. tedious 9. surreptitious 10. tangential

TRUE OR FALSE
1. T 2. F 3. T 4. T 5. T

Lesson 32

MATCHING
1. g 2. f 3. e 4. c 5. i 6. a 7. k 8. d 9. j 10. b

FILL IN THE BLANK
1. thwart or undermine 2. threadbare 3. tenet 4. tentative 5. unassailable
6. undermine 7. tirade 8. turbulence 9. trepidation 10. terse

TRUE OR FALSE
1. T 2. T 3. F 4. T 5. F

Lesson 33

MATCHING
1. f 2. i 3. h 4. b 5. e 6. a 7. d 8. c 9. k 10. g

FILL IN THE BLANK
1. unscathed 2. untenable 3. utopian 4. urbane 5. unethical 6. ungainly
7. vacillate 8. unimpeachable 9. unequivocal 10. unobtrusive

TRUE OR FALSE
1. F 2. T 3. F 4. F 5. T

Lesson 34

MATCHING
1. e 2. h 3. d 4. g 5. i 6. f 7. a 8. k 9. b 10. j

FILL IN THE BLANK
1. verbose 2. validate 3. viable 4. vilify 5. virtuoso 6. vindictive or vitriolic
7. vindictive or vitriolic 8. venerate 9. volatile 10. vicarious

TRUE OR FALSE
1. T 2. F 3. F 4. T 5. F

Lesson 35

MATCHING
1. f 2. d 3. a 4. g 5. h 6. k 7. c 8. b 9. i 10. e

FILL IN THE BLANK
1. waive 2. wanton 3. voracious 4. writhe 5. wither 6. zealot 7. zenith
8. voluminous 9. zany 10. whet

TRUE OR FALSE
1. F 2. F 3. F 4. T 5. F

Review (Lessons 31-35)

ANALOGIES
1. C 2. B 3. E 4. D 5. A 6. D 7. E 8. C 9. A 10. C

ANTONYMS
1. B 2. D 3. B 4. A 5. E 6. C 7. A 8. D 9. C 10. D

HEADLINES
1. susceptible 2. zany 3. tenet 4. utopian 5. unethical 6. virtuoso 7. wither
8. terse 9. talon 10. viable